The Degaev Affair

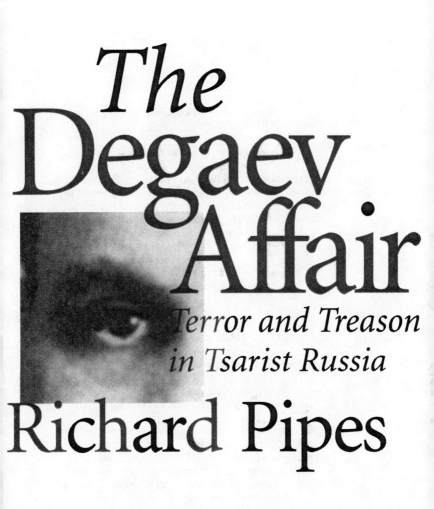

The
Degaev
Affair

Terror and Treason
in Tsarist Russia

Richard Pipes

Yale University Press   *New Haven and London*

Frontispiece: Sergei Degaev, c. 1881
(GARF, Fond 677, opis' 1, delo 1244).

Designed by Sonia Shannon.
Set in Minion type by Tseng Information Systems, Inc.,
Durham, North Carolina.

Library of Congress Cataloging-in-Publication Data
Pipes, Richard.
The Degaev affair : terror and treason in Tsarist Russia /
Richard Pipes.
p. cm.
Includes bibliographical references and index.
ISBN 978-0-300-10772-2
1. Degaev, Sergeæi, 1857–1921.   2. Revolutionaries — Russia —
Biography.   3. Narodnaëiìa volëiìa (Political party : Russia) —
Biography.   4. Russia — History — Alexander III, 1881–1894.
5. Terrorism — Russia.   6. Subversive activities — Russia.
7. Informers — Russia.   8. Internal security — Russia.   I. Title.
DK236.D44 P57   2003
322.4′2′092 — dc21
2002010803

A catalogue record for this book is available
from the British Library.

The paper in this book meets the guidelines for permanence
and durability of the Committee on Production Guidelines
for Book Longevity of the Council on Library Resources.

For who, with us in Russia, is to tell a scoundrel from an exceptionally able man?

—Joseph Conrad, *Under Western Eyes*

Contents

Illustrations

Unless otherwise noted, all illustrations are from GARF, Fond 677, opis' 1, delo 1244.

Preface

My interest in Sergei Degaev–Alexander Pell dates back to the early 1970s, when I first learned about this curious man's double life. The contrast between his behavior in his native Russia, where he triple-crossed his friends and associates, and his conventional academic career in the United States presented a fascinating puzzle. I wondered whether it was due to some peculiar split in his personality or to the vastly different conditions of life in the two countries. The personal mystery gained added importance from the fact that my protagonist played a critical role in destroying the People's Will, the earliest organization devoted to political terrorism and the model for all subsequent terrorist organizations throughout the world.

The great difficulty in studying Degaev-Pell is the shortage of sources. The terrorists and their archfoes, the police authorities, committed as little as possible to paper; much of what documentation existed was burned during the February 1917 revolution, when fires apparently set by secret police agents eager to destroy evidence of their collaboration ravaged the police building in St. Petersburg. As a result, the bulk of the data consists of memoirs of onetime revolutionaries, often strongly biased, especially in the case of the victims of Degaev-Pell's betrayals. Nevertheless, although frustrating, the paucity of primary sources does not preclude tracking my protagonist's actions—although his motivation remains in most cases obscure.

I have been materially helped by several scholars. Jonathan Daly of the University of Illinois at Chicago, an expert on the tsarist police, gave me many valuable hints and answered many of my questions. Feliks Lure of St. Petersburg was also helpful. Marina Pugacheva located for me the relevant documentation in the Moscow State Archive of the Russian Federation (GARF), whose director, Sergei Mironenko, greatly facilitated her work. Zinaida Peregudova helped locate archival documents and photographs. Myriam Lefloch of the Hoover Institution collected for me the materials from the Nikolaevsky Collection at Hoover.

Richard Pipes
Chesham, N.H.
October 2002

Abbreviations

Figner, *Trud*	Vera Figner, *Zapechatlennyi trud,* vol. 1 (Moscow, 1964)
GARF	Gosudarstvennyi Arkhiv Rossiiskoi Federatsii [State Archive of the Russian Federation], Moscow
GM	*Golos Minuvshego*
Granat	*Entsiklopedicheskii slovar' Tov-va Granat,* 55 vols
Hardesty and Unruh	Von Hardesty and John D. Unruh, Jr., "The Enigma of Degaev-Pell," *South Dakota History* 3, no. 1 (Winter 1972), 1–29
KA	*Krasnyi Arkhiv*
KiS	*Katorga i Ssylka*
Kucharzewski, *Od białego caratu*	Jan Kucharzewski, *Od białego caratu do czerwonego,* vol. 7 (Warsaw, 1935)
NChS	*Na Chuzhoi Storone*
Obzor	*Obzor vazhneishikh doznanii proizvodivshikhsia v zhandarmskikh upravleniiakh Imperii po gosudarstvennym prestupleniiam*
Peregudova, *Sysk*	Z. I. Peregudova, *Politicheskii sysk Rossii, 1880–1917* (Moscow, 2000)
Tikhomirov, "V mire"	Lev Tikhomirov, "V mire merzosti zapusteniia," *Vestnik Narodnoi Voli,* no. 2 (1884), Section Sovremennoe Obozrenie, 91–125
Tikhomirov, "Neizdannye"	Lev Tikhomirov, "Neizdannye Zapiski L. Tikhomirova," *Krasnyi Arkhiv,* no. 4/29 (1928), 165–74
VI	*Voprosy Istorii*

The Degaev Affair

CHAPTER ONE

Alexander Pell

The Dakota Territory came into being in 1861. It extended over a vast region of 350,000 square miles — an area equal to that of France and Germany combined — but at the time of its formation it had barely three thousand white settlers, the majority of them concentrated in the southeastern corner, near the Missouri River. The following year, the legislature voted to found in Vermillion, a small town in this enclave, the University of South Dakota, but it failed to appropriate any money for this purpose. In the years that followed, however, the population of the Territory exploded, as hundreds of thousands of new settlers moved in. Twenty-five years later, it had grown to half a million, and the need for higher education became acute. To this end, bonds were issued to secure money for university buildings and faculty salaries.[1]

The university's beginning was rocky. Its first president, the Reverend Ephraim M. Epstein—he was identified in the school's yearbook as "born in Germany of an old Jewish family which claims to trace its descent to Moses"—found the applicants quite unprepared to pursue higher education.[2] After examining them, he decided to admit no one who had not completed elementary grades. At an annual salary of $700, contributed by the citizens of Vermillion, he taught most of the classes himself, combining educational duties with preaching at the local Baptist church. The duties apparently were not to his liking, for he resigned after one year to practice medicine.

After six years—and three presidents—the university had three hundred students, of whom only forty attended college: the others enrolled in the Preparatory Department, which offered a three-year course that provided the equivalent of a high school education. The fourth president, the Norwegian-born Greek scholar Edward Olson, who came to South Dakota in 1887 from the University of Chicago, found the faculty so far below acceptable standards that he felt compelled to dismiss a good part of it. Still, the university grew, although the majority of its students continued to study in the Preparatory Department and never went on to college.

In 1897 the university's Board of Trustees decided that it required a professor of mathematics and turned to Professor Lorrain S. Hulburt of Johns Hopkins for nominees. He responded approximately as follows: "Yes, I have a mathematician for you. He would get a good position almost anywhere here in the East were it not for the Russian brogue with which he speaks. As a mathematician he is first class, and he would accept a position as head of your Department of Mathematics at once." Vermillion's answer was: "Send your Russian mathematician along, brogue and all."[3]

The Russian candidate was a recent Johns Hopkins Ph.D. by the name of Alexander Pell. He arrived in Vermillion in the fall of 1897 with his wife, Emma, to assume duties as the sole professor of mathematics. Of his background, little was known. After he had made himself at home, Pell told his new colleagues that his original name had been Alexander Polevoi; he had adopted his new name on taking U.S. citizenship in 1891. He further informed them that in his youth he had been a "nihilist" and had, on March 1, 1881, personally witnessed the assassination of Alexander II. In time, however, he explained, he had turned his back on nihilism and emigrated. On his subsequent experiences he was somewhat vague. Some sources quoted him as saying he had arrived in the United States "between 1881 and 1886." The 1903 edition of *Coyote*, the University of South Dakota yearbook, stated that he had completed his education in Russia: "After travelling in Europe, he came to America in 1886 and settled in St. Louis, Mo." Moving from place to place, taking on menial jobs while his wife worked as laundress and cook, in October 1895 he enrolled at Johns Hopkins with a major in mathematics and minors in astronomy and English literature. His thirty-four-page dissertation, called *On the Focal Surfaces of the Congruences of Tangents to a Given Surface*, published in Baltimore in 1887, earned him a doctorate.   *ordinary*

In appearance the newcomer was quite unprepossessing: short and stocky, he had reddish hair, a mustache and trimmed beard. He always dressed impeccably. Although he could not rid himself of his Russian "brogue," he made a conscious effort to assimilate. At home, he spoke only English and is said to have voted the Republican ticket. During the Russo-Japanese war of 1904–5 he hoped for a Japanese victory. But he showed little interest in politics.

Pell quickly adapted to the new and unfamiliar environment. Assuming a heavy teaching load, he also took part in a variety of extracurricular activities, including chess and sports: thus he introduced and directed a program of gymnastics for men and women, and faithfully attended the university's athletic contests.

He was highly popular: accounts of him, whether from faculty or students, are uniformly laudatory. The class of 1904 elected him "father" and dedicated its yearbook to him and his wife — only the second time any faculty member was so honored. The March 25, 1901, issue of *Volante*, the school newspaper, reported on Dr. and Mrs. Pell "entertaining the class of which he was class father. From the head of the table beamed the jolly countenance of 'Jolly Little Pell' cracking jokes faster than the freshmen could crack nuts."[4] One alumnus recalled: "Dr. Pell occupied a unique position in the minds and hearts of his students. They respected him profoundly, yet they felt his personal friendship so true that they were at liberty to counsel with him with reference to their personal problems. He was one of the most human men I have ever known."[5] The university's *Alumni Quarterly* said of Pell that he "knew the students in closer good comradeship than any other member of the faculty."[6]

One incident illustrates the reason for his popularity:

At the close of a football game in Mitchell, a group of toughs seized the University colors from a young

Boyd County Public Library

Customer name: STRADER, FRANCES R.
Circulation system messages:
Patron status is ok.

Title: Rod : the autobiography
ID: 33293005567193
Due: 02/04/2013 23:59:59
Circulation system messages:
Item checkout ok.

Total items: 1
1/14/2013 1:07 PM
Checked out: 1
Overdue: 0
Hold requests: 0
Ready for pickup: 0

Circulation system messages:
End Patron Session is successful

Thank you for using the
SelfCheck™ System.

college woman and trampled them in the mud. The wrath of the boys was stirred to patriotic fervor, but a faculty member said to one of them, "Remember to be a gentleman." Alexander Pell, however, vowed that "If a man wants to fight, let him fight." The boys asked, "Who will watch our baggage?" Pell said, "I will," and they went to it. It was bitter, and the college boys were getting the worst of it.

All at once, they saw someone they had never seen before. When he struck a tough, the man went to the ground. The battle was soon over. With victory won, the boys all looked at their champion, his face bloody and his shirt torn to shreds. A youth exclaimed in surprise, "It's Pell."[7]

His loyalty to the school was equaled by his kindness. From his meager annual salary of $1,650 he supported the studies of a young Russian woman, Olga Aleksandrovna Averkieff, who graduated in 1905.[8] He also paid for the medical education at the University of Nebraska of a distant relative, Nina Polevoi.[9]

Pell's true passion was mathematics, which preoccupied his every free moment. His close friend at the university wrote that "one could readily believe that in a social environment where research was the dominating interest Dr. Pell would have been completely satisfied."[10] He published articles in American mathematical journals and attended national mathematical conferences.[11] He was a member of the American Mathematical Society and the Physical-Mathematical Society of Kazan.[12]

He seems eventually to have concluded that a small teach-

Professor Pell and Mrs. Pell in South Dakota

ing university like South Dakota, the majority of whose students attended remedial high school, offered no prospect of advancing pure mathematical scholarship. For this reason six years after his arrival he suggested the creation of an engineering department. After overcoming some resistance, in 1905 he secured the necessary funds to realize his wish. Two years later, the Department of Engineering became the College of Engineering, of which Pell was appointed the first dean.

He was well established — proof that an ex-"nihilist" from cosmopolitan St. Petersburg could successfully assimilate to what was then the American frontier.

No one suspected that "jolly little Pell" — the beloved teacher, the passionate mathematician, the ardent football fan — was in reality Sergei Degaev, a onetime murderer and police informer.

The question that lies at the heart of this book asks which was the true Degaev-Pell: the kindly professor who in America would have been perfectly happy "in a social environment where research was the dominating interest," or the revolutionary turncoat whose betrayals had sent scores of his comrades to prison in his native country and who had killed a man whose confidence he had gained? I can offer no conclusive answer to this question. Not only are the primary sources extremely scarce, but the complexity of human nature is such that when people behave in contradictory ways, it is most difficult to determine which is their true self. As Coleridge has observed, citing the eighteenth-century reformer and philanthropist Samuel Whitbread, no man does anything from a single motive.[13]

Did Degaev-Pell suffer from a split personality? Was his dissimilar behavior on the two continents the natural result of maturation of a man who was in his early twenties when living in Russia, and in his forties when in South Dakota? Or was he perhaps trying in middle age, with good deeds, to atone for the evils he had committed in his youth? Were the conditions of freedom which he encountered in America so different from the ones he had known in Russia as to transform him into a different human being? Or perhaps was Joseph Conrad right in saying that the Russian personality is so enigmatic that a Westerner cannot hope to penetrate it? The reader will have to make up his own mind on the basis of the evidence that follows.

CHAPTER TWO

Sergei Degaev

Everyone seemed to be afraid of something,
everyone seemed to hope for something.

— Andrei Belyi, *Petersburg*

Sergei Degaev was born in Moscow in 1857, the son of Peter Degaev, a military physician, who held the title of State Councillor, which placed him on the fifth level on the Table of Ranks, one level below that which bestowed hereditary nobility. Sergei's mother, Natalie, was the daughter of the well-known writer and historian Nicholas Polevoi. His father seems to have died sometime in the late 1860s, for he played no role in Sergei's mature years. The family consisted of the widowed mother and five children. The eldest daughter, Maria, married an army officer who committed suicide at a young age; Sergei had little contact with her. There were two more sisters living at home: his favorite, Natalie, and Elizabeth (Liza). Natalie later married Nicholas Makletsov, who for a time worked as a mechanic in a brewery, while Liza married his brother, Peter. And finally there was a brother, Vladimir, seven years Sergei's junior.

According to the testimony of people familiar with them, the Degaevs were a "romantic" family, with exalted if unfocused ambitions: like the protagonists of Chekhov plays, they longed for something beyond their reach, something that would transport them to a different, more exhilarating world. According to one acquaintance, "they liked everything unusual and extraordinary."[1] Natalie fancied herself a future actress: at her request, Sergei once invited several prominent revolutionaries for whom she put on a solo performance that was judged an acute embarrassment. A similar reaction met Liza's piano recital.[2] Natalie also conducted spiritual seances at home.[3] According to Vera Figner, a leading revolutionary, another notable trait of the Degaev household was vanity: they always tried to attract attention to themselves, displaying a "tendency to exaggeration, effects and even extravagance." Thus Natalie once boasted of the stir she and Liza had caused in the theater when one appeared in the loge dressed all in white and the other all in black.[4]

Like many if not most middle-class families of the time—for reasons spelled out below—the Degaevs sympathized with the revolutionary movement. They befriended revolutionaries and entertained them at home. In 1881, when the death sentence of the pregnant Gesia Gelfman, one of the ringleaders of the conspiracy to assassinate Alexander II, was commuted to lifelong hard labor, Degaev's mother offered to take care of her child.

Sergei left home at the age of nine to attend the Second Moscow Cadet Corps school; from there he proceeded to the Mikhailovskii Artillery Academy in St. Petersburg. In the academy he struck up acquaintance with radical officers and began to engage in activities which in the eyes of the tsarist authorities were of a subversive nature. In early January 1879, officials of the Third Department of His Majesty's Chancery, then in charge of combating sedition, learned of an incipient industrial strike in the capital city (strikes were illegal in Russia at the time); investigation revealed that the instigators were students from the Artillery Academy. Searches in the quarters which Degaev shared with two other officers unearthed no incriminating evidence, yet it was recommended that they be expelled from the academy on the understanding that their specific guilt would be determined at a later date.[5] Such treatment of young people who engaged in behavior that was perhaps unlawful but hardly threatened the regime—and whose guilt was not even established—assured the revolutionary movement of ever fresh recruits.

Later that year, Degaev retired from active service with the rank of staff captain (*Shtabs Kapitan*), a status between lieutenant and full captain, and enrolled in the Institute of Transport Engineers. There, too, he befriended radicals and before long joined the People's Will, an organization formed in the summer of 1879 for the specific purpose of assassinating the reigning tsar, Alexander II. It was the first organization in history dedicated to systematic political terrorism.

According to the biennial report of the police:

Toward the end of 1880, some students of the Institute of Transport Engineers, infected with an anti-governmental spirit, formed a small circle with the intention of assisting the revolutionary movement which, in their opinion, needed support in view of the numerous arrests carried out in recent years in the ranks of the socialist party. . . . Attending with other students the canteen of the Technological Institute and discussing the means of realizing their plans, in January 1881 they became acquainted with Sergei Degaev, then a student of the Institute of Transport Engineers. Following some meetings, Degaev invited them to the apartment of Cherntsov for a consultation. Having suggested the formation among students of a circle for "self-education," he invited them to meet some of his comrades, best able to grasp revolutionary ideas. . . . On Degaev's advice, all these individuals began to read underground literature, write papers on questions of the greatest interest to them, and then discussed them at gatherings. This activity, which, incidentally, did not go beyond theoretical speculations, attracted the interest also of other students. . . . After a gathering held on March 15, 1881, the circle fell apart, without having realized its plans.[6]

Degaev helped form similar circles at the Artillery Academy from which he had been recently expelled and at the Konstantinov Military School. More important still, he joined the St. Petersburg Central Military Circle, a branch of the People's

Will, formed in the spring of 1880 by A. I. Zheliabov, the mastermind behind the murder of Alexander II.[7] The first two articles of the circle's charter read:

1. The Circle . . . fully shares the program of the party of the People's Will. . . .
2. Forming a branch of the existing revolutionary organization, the Circle, being specifically military, undertakes the following tasks: a) to organize in the army a force for the active struggle against the government, and b) to paralyze the rest of the army which, for whatever reason, is incapable of [waging] an active struggle.[8]

The circle, in addition to Degaev, who did most of the recruiting, consisted of ten to fifteen members; circles formed in other parts of the capital city and its suburbs counted some forty persons.[9]

Thus by the end of 1880 Degaev had become a full-fledged member of the People's Will organization committed to terrorism and revolution.

Opinions of him vary. Some found him personally unimpressive. Figner writes of him that "the main feature which struck one was the complete absence of individuality: there was nothing original, firm and distinguishing about him. Softness, submissiveness were the main qualities that I noticed on first meeting him."[10] Another revolutionary concurs, calling Degaev "colorless."[11] As to his appearance, Figner, who had every reason to despise the man who had delivered her into the hands of the police, says that he did not display that "dumb *(tupoi)* and repulsive expression" of the photographs on the posters offering a reward for his capture. His face was "gentle, good-natured and lively; his manners and voice soft."[12] Indeed, his photograph as a youth shows a person with burning, deep-seated eyes and an alert expression, by no means commonplace. Because of his reticent personality, he adapted easily and readily made friends: one revolutionary described him as "courteous, gentle, sympathetic."[13]

There is unanimity as to his superior intelligence: "My impression of Degaev," wrote one close collaborator, "was that he was very intelligent and knew how to understand and use people. In practical matters, he was remarkably resourceful and clever."[14] Lev Tikhomirov, the leading theoretician of the People's Will, described him as "undoubtedly bright, energetic, with a strong character, but also an inordinately high opinion of himself."[15] Even Figner had to admit that despite his shortcomings, he enjoyed a general reputation for wisdom (though she emphatically did not share it).[16] For all his practical sense, Degaev also showed special aptitude for the abstract — particularly mathematics, which he studied with great passion.

Committed, resourceful, and intelligent, Degaev lacked one quality that the men and women who ran the People's Will valued most of all: the readiness for the sake of the cause to kill in cold blood and to throw his own life away. He suffered from what the revolutionaries contemptuously called "moral squeamishness." He once confessed to a fellow revolutionary that while he was a convinced terrorist, personally he could not commit a terrorist act because "blood frightens him: at the sight of it, he can faint. He said that he could participate indirectly in a terrorist act but in such a manner that he would not witness the inevitable human suffering and blood."[17] Some associates thought him cowardly and accused him of displaying uncontrolled nervousness at the slightest sign of danger. These traits, interpreted as weakness, kept him out of the ranks of the movement's leadership.

Given these facts, the question arises what made Degaev, then in his mid-twenties, risk his freedom and indeed his very life by joining the People's Will. Undoubtedly, ambition played a significant role. In 1880, when he enlisted in the People's Will, the organization was riding high: it seemed to be the wave of the future. Since its formation the previous year, it had carried out several attempts on the life of the tsar, and though all had failed, it was widely believed that when one of them succeeded — as sooner or later it was bound to — the country would erupt in revolution that would sweep away the old order and give Russia a democratic and socialist government that would be the envy of the world. Participation in the revolutionary movement, therefore, carried risks but also the prospect of power and influence in a new Russia. It fitted the "romantic" longings of the Degaev household. Nevertheless, Degaev proved temperamentally unsuited for the kind of life he chose: he experienced constant conflicts between his ambition and his personality which were to cause him no end of grief.

At the time Degaev joined it, the Russian revolutionary movement consisted of three groups. Its core, the so-called Executive Committee of the People's Will, comprised a small band of never more than two dozen fanatical terrorists, many of whom found normal, "bourgeois" existence unbearable. They displayed suicidal tendencies and were prepared — indeed, eager — to sacrifice themselves for the cause so as to give meaning to their otherwise empty lives.[18] The literature on the subject is full of such instances. Thus Tikhomirov recalls meeting two would-be terrorists who insisted on giving up their lives.[19]

Their philosophy was encapsulated in the favorite revolutionary maxim of the time: "The goal justifies the means."[20] They gave no evidence of feeling remorse about killing people who have personally done them no harm: such actions were to them not murders but "executions," and they carried them out with the same calm professionalism as do hangmen enforcing court sentences.

The strange and disturbing feature of the People's Will modus operandi was precisely its habit of "sentencing" people to "execution." The verbs *sentence* and *execute,* of course, come from the vocabulary of law and imply judiciary procedure: crime manifested in violation of the law, trials at which the evidence for and against conviction is presented and weighed, an opportunity for the accused to defend himself. Here no such procedures were observed: people were condemned to death not for what they did but for what they were—namely, representatives of a regime regarded by its very nature to be criminal. The principle of guilt by association was to provide the justification for twentieth-century mass murder in which millions of people would suffer death for no other crime than belonging to a social class or ethnic group that the revolutionaries in power—whether of the communist or the nationalist variety, with the entire state apparatus at their disposal—judged unfit to live. It was a terrible precedent of which the People's Will adherents should have been aware had they given the matter any thought.

The trouble was, they had no opportunity to give thought

Vera Figner

to what they were doing: the task at hand — assassination — was so dangerous and time-consuming that it inhibited reflection. Zheliabov, who organized the murder of Alexander II, said, cryptically, that terror had a "ruinous effect in that it pulled people in against their will."[21] Vera Figner wrote of the "depraving" effect that terrorism had alike on its perpetrators and victims:

> The party proclaimed that all means were good in
> the struggle against the enemy, that in this case the

goal justified the means. At the same time, it fostered the cult of dynamite and the revolver and the glorification of the terrorist. Murder and the gallows acquired a captivating appeal in the minds of youth, and the weaker were their nerves and the harder the life surrounding them, the more did they exult in revolutionary terror. When life offers little so that the results of ideological work are not yet evident, the activist wants to see some concrete, palpable manifestation of his will, his power. Such manifestation at that time could be only a terrorist act with its violence.[22]

Lev Tikhomirov, the theorist of revolutionary terror, described, after he had broken with the revolutionaries, the lot to which the terrorist condemned himself:

The very way of life of the terrorist has a stupefying effect. It is the life of a hunted wolf. The dominant awareness is that he must be prepared to perish not just today or tomorrow, but any second. The only hope of coping with this awareness is to push out of mind many matters which for someone who wishes to be a mature human being require thought. In this condition, an attachment of any seriousness and of any kind is a genuine misfortune. The study of any question or social phenomenon is unthinkable. A plan of action, minimally complex, minimally comprehensive, is not even allowed to enter one's mind. Apart from five to ten like-minded persons, one must deceive from morning to night literally everyone; one must hide from everyone, suspect in everyone an enemy. . . . One needs extraordinary fortitude to think and work at all under such unnatural conditions. But even those who possess it, unless they extricate themselves from the quagmire of their situation, quickly go under. For individuals of lesser caliber, these perpetual intrigues with spies, false passports, conspiratorial apartments, dynamites, ambushes, dreams of murders, escapes prove even more disastrous.[23]

Supporting the actual terrorists was a larger body of individuals prepared to risk freedom to facilitate their work whether by providing shelter, raising money, printing manifestos and other illegal publications, recruiting agents and rendering other services short of personally committing acts of terrorism. If caught — unless prepared to betray their comrades — they usually received long-term sentences of imprisonment or hard labor. This was the category to which belonged Sergei Degaev.

Almost all in the first category and most in the second were young. The Russian revolutionary movement was a distinctly youthful phenomenon; its active members were usually in their twenties, sometimes thirties, occasionally teens, hardly ever forty or older. As such, it displayed the typical characteristics of youth movements: loyalty to the group and willingness to sacrifice oneself for it were considered supreme values, superseding not only self-interest but also broader ethical considerations.

Finally, there was society at large, consisting of the coun-

Lev Tikhomirov

try's educated and affluent elite, the great majority of which, according to the testimony of contemporaries, sympathized with the terrorists, providing them with moral and financial support. It is surprising to what extent this group, that half a century later was to be the principal victim of the revolution — losing its properties if not lives, suffering abuse and humiliation, as well as imprisonment or expulsion from the country — collaborated in its own destruction. We have to this effect the testimony of no less an authority than Vladimir Burtsev, the historian of the Russian revolution and a onetime member of the People's Will:

Society, and youth especially and in particular, opposed the government. The government, apart from its bureaucracy and army, which stood aside from politics, enjoyed no support and was estranged from the entire country. Its estrangement from society was such that even in law-abiding circles all and each derived malicious pleasure from whatever had the smallest bearing on state authority. . . .

Although Platonic, undoubtedly there was overall sympathy for the revolutionaries. By the way, and perhaps even in particular, this manifested itself in general sympathy for political terror and, specifically, for attempts on the life of the tsar. The terrorists expressed social protest. More than that — they embodied society's hope. People wanted and expected terror. If they sometimes felt indignant at the terrorists it was only because they were unsuccessful in their actions or altogether failed to act. News of attempts on the life of the tsar . . . were greeted with unconcealed joy. Many who had nothing in common with the terrorists and the revolutionaries in general went to meet them halfway. . . .

Terror was welcomed not only by extreme left-wing circles but also by moderate ones. No one in society dared to condemn the terrorists. This was done only by such reactionaries whom no one trusted.[24]

This judgment, supported by other evidence, provides a devastating condemnation of Russia's elite of the time, and suggests that far from invariably defending their own interests and using the state to this end, as Marxism would have it, the propertied class is perfectly capable of doing everything in its power to destroy itself.

The prorevolutionary sympathies of the educated and propertied are the more astonishing in that the program of the People's Will explicitly referred to these groups as partners and beneficiaries of Russia's despotic regime which it was determined to overthrow.

Several explanations suggest themselves for this behavior. One was compassion for the young who sacrificed themselves for what they claimed to be the common good. Ivan Turgenev, a skeptic and a liberal, was so impressed by the deed of the twenty-eight-year old Vera Zasulich—who had shot the commandant of St. Petersburg as revenge for his order to whip an imprisoned student who had refused to take off his hat in the commandant's presence—that he glorified her in *Senilia*, his "Poems in Prose," in a sketch called "Threshold." Here, a young girl about to commit a political crime is warned of all the penalties she will suffer. Yet she is willing to do so and with open eyes crosses the threshold that leads to crime and punishment. "Fool!" someone shouts. "Saint!" another replies. Even the archreactionary Fyodor Dostoevsky, for whom revolutionaries were possessed by demons, once admitted in private conversation that if he accidentally overheard a discussion among revolutionaries plotting a terrorist act, he would not report it to the police to prevent the crime.*

*Cited in Isaiah Berlin, *Russian Thinkers* (New York, 1978), 304–5. The person to whom Dostoevsky made this confession, the archconservative newspaper editor A. S. Suvorin, agreed that he too would keep quiet.

Another factor behind society's sympathy for the terrorists was the conviction that the tsarist government was so sturdy that no amount of rebellion could shake it, but that it might yet be forced to grant the country the liberties which it desperately needed. Some of the more sophisticated liberals then and later welcomed terrorism as a means of pressure on the government which alone would compel it to give up autocracy. Few realized until it was too late how tenuous was the authority of the tsarist regime and how powerful the destructive forces that lurked behind the facade of rigidity and order.

The Russian revolutionary movement began innocently enough. In the 1860s, when the relatively enlightened Alexander II relaxed the autocratic regime that under his father, Nicholas I, had made Russia the most illiberal country in Europe, the opposition, centered on the universities, confined its resistance to ideology. The "sons," rejecting the idealism and romanticism of the generation of their "fathers," swung toward extreme forms of positivism and utilitarianism, which attributed reality only to that which was empirically verifiable and value only to that which conferred the greatest happiness of the greatest number. It rejected all ideas and institutions that failed to meet these criteria. Nihilism, as the movement came to be known in the early 1860s, insisted on challenging every aspect of social reality, hoping, by opening minds, to make possible fundamental change for the better. In practice, this expressed itself mainly in the study of the natural sciences and the criticism of the status quo from the scientific point of view.

In the early 1870s youth turned from study to action. The emancipation of the serfs by Alexander II in 1861 had liberated tens of millions of men and women who previously had been little more than chattel. This new situation seemed to offer unprecedented opportunities to infuse progressive ideas into the masses and in this manner to stir them into action against the autocracy. In 1874 as many as one thousand university students abandoned their classrooms and went "to the people" — some to agitate for immediate rebellion, others to spread positivist and utilitarian ideas that, by making the common people aware of the injustice of the status quo, would plant seeds of rebellion in their minds. The revolutionary youth had unbounded faith in the wisdom of Russia's common people and did not doubt that, once enlightened, they would form an invincible army that would crush the whole wretched regime based on oppression and exploitation.

Disenchantment came soon enough. The peasant, it turned out on closer contact, was at heart not a rebel but a monarchist. He believed that the tsar literally owned Russia and that hence he and he alone was in a position to satisfy his principal grievance, the shortage of land. Of this attitude there are numerous examples in the memoirs of contemporary radicals, of which the following is typical. A participant in the "going to the people" movement describes how he and two of his comrades settled in a village disguised as carpenters with the intention of spreading socialist propaganda. They would strike up conversations with peasants to enlighten them about the injustice of their condition. On one occasion, in answer to a question how people lived in foreign countries, they described, in Marxist terms, how the English enclosure acts had led to the expulsion of farmers from the land. The peasants, having listened attentively, responded: yes, abroad things are truly bad because the lords *(pany)* had taken possession of all the land. The same would happen in Russia were it not for the tsar. We have little land, they complained, but "the tsar will give. Absolutely. There is nothing doing without land. Who will pay the taxes? Who will fill the treasury? And without the treasury, how can you rule? The land will be ours! Ab-so-lu-te-ly! You will see!" In sum, the peasants concluded that "under the tsar, we have it much better than other people, where the lords run everything."[25] The radical "propagandists," appalled by such an unexpected response, were forced to conclude that instead of destroying the people's illusions they had merely strengthened their faith in the tsar.

Various tactics were tried to change the peasant mentality, but to no avail: the peasants remained steadfast in their trust in tsarism and the benefits it would bring them. In some localities, they turned over the student agitators and propagandists to the authorities, who subsequently tried them for subversive activity. In one notorious instance, when the peasants did respond to radical agitation by rebelling against their landlords, it transpired that they had been told the tsar desired them to do so.

The reactions to this disappointment varied. Some radical youths abandoned the movement and went back to their studies. A small group, who emigrated to Switzerland, adopted Social Democracy and the Marxist tenet that revolution, as the social consequence of economic development, is inevitable but not to be rushed. Yet another group drew from this experience the lesson that no progress was attainable in Russia until the reverential awe in which the population at large held the tsar and his regime had been shattered: and the way to secure this end was to proceed beyond propaganda and agitation to involvement in politics, by which was meant a campaign of assassinations directed at the monarch and his officials. Activity of this kind would demonstrate to the rural and urban masses the vulnerability of the regime and encourage them to take matters into their own hands.

Such was the strategy adopted in late summer 1879 by a small group of radicals at a clandestine meeting held in a forest near the town of Lipetsk. There they formed the organization which they named People's Will: the name can be explained only by the belief that the twenty or so intellectuals who founded the organization were the true "people" and hence entitled to speak and act in the nation's name.* The Executive Committee, which at its founding was the whole organization, later that year adopted a program calling for the spread of socialist ideas and, concurrently, the pursuit of terror. The latter was justified on the following grounds: "Terrorist activity, which aims at the elimination of the most harmful government personalities, the protection of the party from spies, the punishment of the most glaring instances of violence and arbitrariness on part of the government [and] the administration etc. — has as its objective undermining the fascination with state power, providing an uninterrupted demonstration of the feasibility of fighting the government, in this manner awakening the revolutionary spirit of the people and their belief in the success

---

* The Russian word for will — *volia* — also means unrestrained freedom, and some historians translate *Narodnaia volia* as People's Freedom. But contemporary evidence makes it clear that the name given the organization was meant to convey the idea of will.

of the cause, and, finally, mustering suitable forces, accustomed to combat."[26]

The Lipetsk meeting "sentenced" Alexander II to death, entrusting the mission to the Executive Committee. Initially this committee consisted of some ten members: although it expanded in time, its membership never exceeded twenty or so. The designation was as much of a misnomer as the name of the organization it headed. The Executive Committee did not carry out decisions made by its membership; on the contrary, it issued orders to its constituents, who were duty bound to obey them unquestioningly. Free of any external controls, it was, in a sense, a mirror image of tsarism. It was organized on a strictly centralized model, with all decisions flowing from the top downward; members had to be willing to sacrifice for the cause everything they valued—friendships, personal loyalties, freedom, indeed their very lives. Both structure and esprit of the People's Will were to provide two decades later a model for Lenin's Bolshevik Party.*

The execution of the "sentence" passed on Alexander II took longer than anticipated, namely a year and a half. It was finally crowned with success on March 1, 1881. The results were paltry in the extreme: the masses did not stir. In fact, not a few peasants interpreted the assassination of the monarch as revenge by the landlords for the abolition of serfdom and voiced fear that with his death the Emancipation Edict would be rescinded.[27] The sweeping arrests carried out just before and after

---

* Lenin's elder brother, Alexander, a member of the People's Will, was executed in 1887 for participation in a plot to assassinate Alexander III.

March 1 decimated the organization, although it managed to carry on and even to convey the impression that it was as strong as ever.

The unprecedented terror campaign launched by the People's Will attracted the attention of all Europe: Marx himself, for all his insistence that revolutions could not be made but had to happen, conceded that, of all countries, in Russia it was possible for a small group of determined radicals to seize power and carry out a revolution from above.

It is tempting to attribute the mounting violence of the Russian revolutionary movement to the conditions under which Russians were compelled to live. For, indeed, Russia at the time was an oppressive country, especially so for the educated elite. According to the Criminal Code of 1845:

1. All attempts to limit the authority of the sovereign, or to alter the prevailing system of government, as well as to persuade others to do so, or to give overt expression to such intentions, or to conceal, assist, or fail to denounce anyone guilty of these offenses, carry the death penalty and the confiscation of all property;

2. The spreading by word of mouth or by means of the written or printed word of ideas which, without actually inciting to sedition, as defined above, *raise doubts about the authority of the sovereign or lessen respect for him or his office,* are punishable *by the loss of civil rights and terms of hard labor from four to twelve years, as well as corporal punishment and branding.*[28]

These provisions, in force until the revolution of 1905, in effect prohibited under severe penalties any questioning of the political status quo. In other words, the autocracy was subject neither to laws nor to control by representative bodies. For the vast majority of the population—some 90 percent peasants or manual workers—this hardly mattered. But it created insufferable conditions for people who traveled abroad and familiarized themselves with Western political and sociological literature, because any aspiration for political change, if publicly expressed, was treated as a crime.

In view of these facts, it may be natural to explain—and justify—the emergence of a violent revolutionary movement as a natural reaction to intolerable conditions. But are matters really that simple: is violence bred of despotism? or, as is sometimes, argued, of poverty? If it were so, then there should be no political violence in prosperous countries which guarantee personal freedoms and the rule of law. Such was the reaction of the Executive Committee of the People's Will to the assassination in the United States in 1881 of President James Garfield, when it sent to the American people a letter of condolences protesting this act of terrorism: "In a country where individual freedom offers opportunities for honest ideological struggle, where the free will of the nation determines not only the law but also the personality of those who govern—in such a country, political assassination as a means of struggle is a manifestation of the same despotic spirit, the destruction of which in Russia is our goal. . . . Violence is justified only when it is directed against violence."[29]

And yet, in the United States, a country which was everything tsarist Russia was not, rich and as free and law-abiding as any society in history, a similar movement arose in the 1960s and 1970s. This movement also resorted to terrorism and aimed at the overthrow of the status quo for the sake of a society which would know neither "capitalism" nor "imperialism" nor "racism." And in Germany of the late 1960s — also prosperous, democratic, and law-abiding — there came into being the so-called Red Army Faction, led by the Baader-Meinhof gang, which abducted and killed in cold blood prominent business-men as symbols of "capitalism." Together with other terrorist gangs in Germany, the RAF was responsible for some two hun-dred deaths. A poll conducted in 1971 revealed that one-fourth of Germans under thirty expressed "a certain sympathy" for the Red Army Faction. And twenty years later, "terrorist chic" was all the fashion.[30]

These facts suggest that revolutionary violence is not en-tirely or even mainly inspired by political oppression and/or poverty. For some dimly understood reason, in modern soci-eties from time to time, a sizable body of the young is seized by an overpowering destructive urge which, at the same time, exhibits self-destructive symptoms. When this happens, the os-tensible objective — an ideal political and social order — serves but as a pretext for resort to violence: violence, ostensibly the means to an end, becomes an end in itself. The presumed ob-jective merely legitimizes behavior that otherwise would be judged purely criminal. And since in our imperfect world there are always matters that can be improved, "causes" can always be found to justify the urge to destroy and murder.

Having joined the People's Will in the winter of 1880–81 and organized clandestine cells in St. Petersburg, Degaev thought he had earned for himself a place on its Executive Committee, and in February 1881 he asked to be admitted. Such a request was considered bad form, for the committee chose its members not by application but by co-optation in accordance with its own criteria. His request was rejected. He took it hard, and complained of feeling "insulted"; despite his contribution to the cause and his reliability in carrying out orders from above, he was considered unworthy of membership in the directing organ. The committee responded that while it trusted and valued him, it thought him insufficiently "revolutionary."[31] To demonstrate his commitment, he was asked to take part in the nighttime digging of a tunnel under Malaia Sadovaia street intended for a mine that was to be exploded when the tsar's carriage passed over it. He complied. Whether he actually witnessed the tsar's murder by a thrown bomb on March 1, as he later graphically related to his friends in South Dakota, cannot be established. What is known is that on April 21, 1881, in the sweep of radicals carried out after this event, having come under police observation for some time, he was incarcerated in the House of Preliminary Detention. No incriminating evidence against him came to light, the more so that he could prove that he was too busy with his perfectly legitimate occupations with which he supported his family to have time for revolutionary activity—so on May 5 he was released on bail of two thousand rubles.[32]

He returned to his studies and in June graduated from the Institute of Transport Engineers, following which he left for Archangel in the far north to take an engineering job. There he met his future wife, Liubov Nikolaevna Ivanova, by all accounts a simple woman, three years younger, who had some casual contacts with local revolutionary circles. It was love at first sight. Degaev immediately proposed to her, but she did not wish to marry before attending midwife's school in St. Petersburg, where she moved in August. Degaev returned to St. Petersburg in November, and they married. Degaev and his wife were genuinely devoted to each other throughout their marriage, which lasted until her death twenty-three years later.

CHAPTER THREE

Lieutenant Colonel Sudeikin

Degaev might have ended up as a short footnote in the history of the Russian revolutionary movement had not there appeared at this point in his life the mysterious and sinister figure of Georgii Porfirevich Sudeikin, the head of Russia's security services. By devising new and sophisticated methods of police investigation, Sudeikin influenced decisively the procedures of Russian security organs not only during the remaining decades of tsarism but also those of the Soviet Union. As did most members of the imperial political police, Sudeikin threw a veil of secrecy over his personal life. He succeeded so well in concealing information about himself that for more than a century after his death next to nothing was known about his past:

his photographic likeness was first made public in 2000. Apart from his formal service record and a few scraps of writings, virtually all the information about him comes from recollections of revolutionaries.

Sudeikin was born on April 11, 1850, in the Smolensk province in an impoverished and landless gentry family.[1] After completing secondary schooling, he volunteered for the army. From 1868 to 1870 he attended the Infantry Cadet School in Moscow, from which he graduated with top honors and then went on active army service as an ensign. The following year he was promoted to second lieutenant.

In 1874 Sudeikin requested to be transferred from the army to the Corps of Gendarmes, the service responsible for maintaining order and preventing sedition. In so doing, he followed the pattern of many impecunious nobles, as Jonathan W. Daly has written: "Ambitious young men from gentry families who could not aspire to enter the elite guards units often hoped to serve in the Gendarme Corps, which to many of them seemed more glamorous and prestigious than the regular military service."[2] Their salary was at least twice that of ordinary officers and they wore handsome blue uniforms.[3]

But in Sudeikin's case another motive seems to have played a part as well. Imaginative and audacious, he was fascinated by adventure stories, especially those dealing with crime and detection. He is said to have been especially infatuated with the popular detective novels of the mid-nineteenth-century French writer Emile Gaboriau.[4] Gaboriau's hero, Lecoq, was a poor but ambitious orphan lad who saw no chance for himself in the world. He found employment with a prominent astronomer, Baron Moser, but after five years of toil, for which

Georgii Sudeikin

he received a mere one hundred francs a month, he felt disheartened: "He was nearly crazed with rage and disappointment when he recapitulated his blighted hopes, his fruitless efforts, and the insults he had endured." In this mood, he fantasized about acquiring a fortune by criminal means. He confided to his employer a plan he had conceived of obtaining money without risk of exposure or failure. The baron, impressed by the ingenuity of Lecoq's scheme, decided nevertheless to dismiss him because he thought it unwise to employ so cunning a secretary. Having paid him his salary a month in advance, he told Lecoq, "When one has your disposition, and is poor, one may either become a famous thief or a great detective. Choose."

> Lecoq retired in confusion; but the astronomer's words bore fruit in his mind. "Why should I not follow good advice?" he asked himself. Police service did not inspire him with repugnance — far from it. He had often admired that mysterious power whose hand is everywhere, and which, although unseen and unheard, still manages to hear and see everything. He was delighted with the prospect of being the instrument of such a power. He considered that the profession of detective would enable him to employ the talents with which he had been endowed in a useful and honorable fashion; besides opening out a life of thrilling adventure with fame as its goal.[5]

From what we know of Sudeikin, such considerations very likely played an important part in his decision, at the age of twenty-three, to become a gendarme. His objective was not only money but also power and adventure. In the words of a high Russian official, "for him the war with the nihilists resembled a hunt . . . the contest of skill and cunning, the danger, the satisfaction from success."[6] He was intrigued by the criminal mind and it seems that the only serious literature that he read dealt with this subject. Lev Tikhomirov, while giving due to Sudeikin's abilities as police official, noted that he "had no convictions, and treated with complete indifference human suffering, happiness or unhappiness."[7] A one-time terrorist, Stepniak-Kravchinskii, called him a "political chameleon."[8] Indeed, as Sudeikin told some of the revolutionaries whom he interrogated, he could just as readily have been one of them: principles and convictions played in his case no part. He once said, only half in jest, that if "the Russian revolutionary party disposed of such means of compensating its agents [as the government], I would serve it just as loyally."[9] He spoke with approval of terrorist assaults on such "scum" as the Governor of Kharkov, Prince Dmitrii Kropotkin, and F. F. Trepov, the city commandant of St. Petersburg and the victim of Vera Zasulich's bullet. He also praised Zheliabov as a "great man," and his companion, Sophia Perovskaia, as a "saint."[10] He loved the game for its own sake. Because he was telling the truth, his words carried conviction and played no small part in his remarkable ability to secure his victims' cooperation.

While working for the monarchy with zeal and at great personal risk, he held it in low esteem. When he presented himself to imprisoned revolutionaries as a "constitutionalist" or even "socialist"—on one occasion he boasted that he had learned from revolutionaries about the teachings of Marx— he was not entirely dissimulating.[11] He treated his position as an exciting job rather than an ideological or political commitment. His victims concur that he displayed no personal hostility toward them and did not treat them cruelly.

At the same time, he was well aware of the risks he was running. He is quoted as saying that he expected to be assassinated but hoped to postpone the inevitable for as long as possible.[12] To elude assassins, he led a highly irregular life. Aware that the revolutionaries wanted to eliminate him as their most dangerous enemy, he conducted himself not unlike his adversary, the professional terrorist: the hunter was also the quarry. He carried several passports, all in different names, wore different uniforms, maintained several residences, which he would abandon after a few weeks,[13] and usually met his agents at odd hours in hired cabs or suburban cottages rather than in his office at Gorokhovaia 2. According to one source, he lodged his family in an apartment in one of the St. Petersburg prisons.[14]

In 1877, having been three years earlier promoted to the rank of staff captain, Sudeikin was posted to Kiev, a major center of revolutionary activity. After the gendarme officer G. E. Geiking was assassinated in Kiev in May 1870, Sudeikin took his place. He quickly distinguished himself by his skill in uncovering revolutionary plots. An indefatigable worker, he acquired a reputation for bravery by personally leading an assault on the headquarters of an armed terrorist group, and in February 1879 by apprehending virtually all Kievan revolutionaries, including the southern Executive Committee of the People's Will.[15] These operations for the time being virtually wiped out the terrorist cells in southern Russia.

His accomplishments attracted the attention of the authorities in St. Petersburg, still recovering from the shock that followed the murder of Alexander II and in a panic over the prospect of terrorist outrages against the murdered tsar's son and successor, Alexander III. In July 1881, on the recommendation of V. S. Strelnikov, the military procurator for the southern region, Sudeikin was transferred to the capital city and charged with responsibility for maintaining public order there. With him came his wife, Vera Petrovna, née Guseva, the daughter of a colonel in the Corps of Gendarmes, and two children, a son Leonid, age four, and a daughter Sofia, two years old. (A second son, Sergei, was born in March 1882).

The tsarist government was poorly equipped to fight the revolution. In 1883, for example, the Moscow branch of the Okhrana — one of the several security organizations established to combat sedition — numbered a mere twenty-six surveillance officers and eleven secret agents.[16] They were quite ineffective in that they concentrated on penalizing rather than preventing political crimes. The apparent assumption was that severe punishment — execution by hanging, confinement to solitary cells in fortress prisons, or hard labor in Siberia — would serve as a deterrent. It failed to do so, and the revolutionaries continued their destructive work.

Sudeikin concluded that such reactive procedures were futile. To prevent political crimes, he decided, required that the war be carried into the enemy camp by penetrating revolutionary circles and sowing confusion in their ranks. He would bore from within, hoping to demoralize the radical underground to the point where it would destroy itself. To this end he employed various means, but they all rested on a cynical view of mankind: "I always count on human weakness," he was quoted as saying.[17]

On assuming his new post, Sudeikin created a department, separate from the investigative agency, which was to exert "active influence" on the revolutionaries. Its functions were

1. To instigate, with the help of special active collaborators, quarrels and disputes among diverse revolutionary groups;
2. To spread false rumors [to] threaten and terrorize the revolutionary milieu;
3. To transmit, through the same agents and occasionally with the assistance of persons on short-term arrests called in by the police, accusations that the most dangerous revolutionaries were spying [for the police], and, at the same time, to discredit revolutionary proclamations and various printed organs [by depicting them] as provocations of the secret police.[18]

Sudeikin owed his meteoric rise in the police establishment to the application of such refined methods of infiltration, surveillance, and investigation. For one, he was the first to create a network of informants who reported to him on the intentions of revolutionaries, enabling him to forestall terrorist attacks.[19] Unlike his predecessors, he did not arrest revolutionaries as soon as he had identified them; instead, following French practice, he left them at liberty until such time as persistent observation had revealed to him the circle of their associates. Only when the entire network became known did he carry out arrests.

Once they were in his power, Sudeikin divided the revolutionaries into two categories: the corrupt and the naive. The former he sought to win over with money and/or release from prison, the latter with appeals to idealism. Gifted with keen psychological insight, he quickly determined which approach was most likely to secure a prisoner's collaboration.*

He was lavish with money, paying liberal allowances to anyone he knew to have connections with revolutionary circles, whether or not the beneficiary repaid him with information. At one time, more than fifty students at St. Petersburg University were on his payroll, a fact they readily confessed to each other, treating it as a joke.[20] Such reactions did not trouble him in the least; he felt confident his generosity would pay off sooner or later: "Let him take! The more he takes the more difficult it will be later to distinguish a [police] agent from a revolutionary. Anyway, for a few months he will take and give nothing, and then we will get something out of him."[21]

For more principled revolutionaries who could not be bought off, he used a sophisticated psychological approach, assuring them that he was on their side and shared their loathing of the existing regime. He went to great lengths—and had considerable success—in persuading his prisoners, especially the youngest, most idealistic ones, to help him prevent terrorist outrages, his principal concern. In cordial conversations, he would insist that terrorism was entirely counterproductive, thwarting reforms and playing into the hands of reactionaries. The terrorists could attain their ultimate objective—reforming Russia—far better by working with progressive officials like

---

*With workers whom the radicals won over, he used still another approach, telling them that they had been misled by the intellectuals: he tended to release them and give them money to find work. Tikhomirov, "V mire," 111.

himself. He did not invent this particular approach, but he practiced it on a scale and with a skill that had no precedent.

The kind of relationship which Sudeikin was seeking to establish with the revolutionary underground was only partly a police measure designed to deceive and disarm. The government, with its rudimentary and understaffed police apparatus, was terrified of the People's Will, whose strength it tended wildly to exaggerate. It saw "nihilists" everywhere. As one of the Grand Dukes, describing "general panic," wrote after a revolutionary, disguised as a worker, had smuggled dynamite into the Winter Palace and exploded it under the imperial dining room: "We are living through a period of terror with only this difference that during the [French] revolution Parisians saw their enemies, while we not only do not see and do not know our enemies but even have no idea how many of them there are."[22] So frightened was the new tsar, Alexander III, of the invisible enemy that, apart from attending his father's funeral, he stayed out of sight in Gatchina, twenty-five miles outside the capital city, which was guarded around the clock like a prison.[23] The capital city was placed under a state of siege. The coronation was postponed indefinitely.

To cope with the danger, the government made several tentative efforts to reach an understanding with the revolutionaries. Thus, late in 1881, Viacheslav Plehve, the head of the newly formed Police Department, asked an arrested terrorist to state the conditions under which the People's Will would suspend its campaign of violence. On another occasion, jointly with Sudeikin, Plehve offered to arrange for the escape of an imprisoned revolutionary if, in return, he would try to avert terrorist violence.[24] Separately, similar negotiations were carried out by the so-called Holy Brotherhood, a private counterterrorist organization of government supporters, and another group which called itself Voluntary Okhrana. This group requested that the Executive Committee lift its "death sentence" on Alexander III, by which action it might persuade the government to introduce a constitutional regime.[25] None of these feelers produced any results because the demands of the Executive Committee of the People's Will were nonnegotiable. A few days after the death of Alexander II, it addressed a letter to his successor in which it insisted, among other concessions, on the convocation of a representative body that would "review the existing forms of political and social life and their transformation in accord with popular wishes" — in other words, abdication.[26]

This meant that the war had to go on. And the most promising strategy was that employed by Sudeikin: penetrating the People's Will and destroying it from within.

The approach used by Sudeikin, which enabled him to "turn around" not a few revolutionaries and ultimately to destroy their organization, had been devised by the Odessa deputy procurator, A. F. Dobrzhinskii, and first tested by him on an imprisoned terrorist named Grigorii Goldenberg.[27]

Goldenberg was born in 1855 in Berdichev in an affluent Orthodox Jewish family. As a youth he abandoned his family's religion and established contacts with revolutionaries, eventually turning into a fanatical terrorist. In February 1879 he assassinated the governor of Kharkov, Prince Dmitrii Kropotkin. Having eluded arrest, that June he attended the secret gathering at Lipetsk which created the People's Will and was elected to its Executive Committee. He volunteered to assassinate Alexander II but was dissuaded on the grounds that it would be unwise for this to be done by a Jew.

On November 14, 1879, Goldenberg was apprehended in Elizavetgrad with a suitcase full of nitroglycerine, which he intended to deliver to associates in Moscow to blow up a train carrying the tsar. Incarcerated in Odessa, for two months he was left alone, after which he was interrogated by Dobrzhinskii. The questioning was friendly. The deputy procurator did not threaten or pressure his prisoner but unfolded before him a seductive picture of the glorious future in store for Russia once it was no longer threatened by terrorism. Goldenberg, who even before his arrest had lived under intense emotional stress — he described himself as "spiritually sick" — now suffered bouts of severe anxiety that brought him to the brink of a nervous breakdown. This condition was caused less by Dobrzhinskii's alluring prospects than by the feeling that the revolutionary movement was doomed and that further terrorist attacks would achieve nothing except claim ever more lives. Murder — whether assassination of government officials or death by hanging of the assassins — struck him now as a monstrous crime which had to be stopped at all costs.

Goldenberg began to experience nightmares, haunted by the image of hangings. His jailers, aware of his precarious mental state, entered with him into a dialogue. They succeeded in convincing him that they wished nothing but good for Russia's youth and loved their country as much as did he and his comrades. Goldenberg agreed with them that it was in everyone's interest to stop political assassinations and, along with them, death sentences. To this end, in March 1880 he was persuaded to divulge what he knew of the People's Will organization. He realized full well that those whom he was betraying would be punished, but consoled himself with the thought that they would suffer nothing more harsh than a few years of exile: the hangings would stop. As he later wrote in his "Confession": "Once I had resolved these issues, it seemed to me that there was no happier human being. I imagined that in this manner I had become the savior of all youth and all comrades. It seemed to me that I was making a sacrifice such as the world had never witnessed, that I risked the entire reputation, the entire good and honest name that I enjoyed among my comrades, only in order to save them from inevitable death."[28]

In this frame of mind verging on delirium, Goldenberg became a police collaborator. He was subsequently transferred to St. Petersburg (followed by Dobrzhinskii) and incarcerated in the dreaded Trubetskoi Bastion of the Peter-Paul Fortress. There, in mid-April, he had a visit from M. T. Loris-Melikov, appointed dictator of the empire to combat terror, who chatted with him in a friendly manner.[29]

Imprisoned Russian revolutionaries had developed in 1875 an ingenious code which permitted them to communicate from their solitary cells through the prison walls. A chart of thirty squares—five numbered horizontally and six vertically—accommodated all the letters of the Russian alphabet. Thus, the letter *m* was conveyed by three taps (vertical scale) followed by two (horizontal scale). This code enabled political prisoners, most of the time, to frustrate the efforts of their jailers to isolate them from each other.[30]

Before long, from conversations with other inmates carried out in this manner, Goldenberg came to realize that he had been duped: the information he had provided served to decimate revolutionary ranks without having any effect on government policy. In the first half of 1880 the executions continued unabated. Despondent, he wrote his "Confession," an amazing document of a wretched young man trying to justify himself, and on July 15, 1880, he hanged himself in his cell by tying a towel around his neck and suspending it from the duct of the wash basin.

When Alexander II learned of Goldenberg's suicide, he wrote of a man who only a few months before had been prepared to assassinate him: "Ochen' zhal'!" — A great pity![31]

Sudeikin adopted Dobrzhinskii's methods. He would let a prisoner spent some time in a solitary cell until suitably "softened," and then conduct an interrogation either in his office or in prison.

Russian prisons of the time, particularly Schlüsselburg and Peter-Paul, the two converted fortresses in the capital city used to confine the most dangerous political criminals, were forbidding places. The Russian revolutionary Stepniak-Kravchinskii described it for readers in England, where he had taken refuge:

> When night falls upon the capital and thousands of lights illumine the quays of the Neva, the [Peter-Paul] fortress alone remains in darkness, like a huge black maw ever open to swallow up all the noblest and most generous of the unhappy country that it rules. No living sound comes to break the grim silence that hangs over this place of desolation. . . .

Every quarter of an hour the prison clock repeats a tedious irritating air, always the same, a psalm in praise of God and the Tzar. . . .

The fortress is . . . an absolutely cellular prison. It is composed of bastions, curtains, ravelins, like all fortresses built on the Vauban system. Each of these divisions forms a separate prison, with its own director, its body of gaolers and gendarmes, who are lodged separately and rarely communicate with one another. Each of these prisons consists of a certain number of cells, distributed over two floors, large enough to accommodate several hundreds of prisoners. The most minute watch is kept to prevent these prisoners from communicating. They never meet, never speak to one another, and if they see each other it is only at a distance. . . . For greater safety, [the warders are] prohibited to answer the questions of any prisoner, no matter how innocent. A question about the weather, the day of the week, receives no answer from the gaolers. Silently they approach the grating of your door, silently they bring the bread and soup. At the hour for exercise they silently open your cell, and without a word lead you to the court yard, or rather a small compartment of the yard, a kind of roofless cell, where you walk up and down, seeing only the four walls, and a small piece of sky overhead. Then you are led back to your sad cell as silently as you were brought out. There is thus absolute isolation, the isolation of

A cell in the Peter-Paul Fortress

death, in the place full of human beings, all suffering alike.[32]

"Silence, eternal silence," recalled Vera Figner of her long sojourn in the Schlüsselburg fortress: "From inactivity, the vocal cords weakened, atrophied; the voice broke, disappeared. . . . This physical derangement of the speech organ was accompanied by changes in the mental state. . . . Apart from compelling necessity . . . one felt like keeping silent, and when one had to say something, it took an effort of the will."[33]

Isolated from everything alive, many prisoners went mad. Some others, after a few months of such seclusion, were ready to pay any price to regain their freedom or at least reestablish contact with humanity. Sudeikin would usually allow them time in their dark and silent cells before coming up with an offer of collaboration. A prisoner reported from Peter-Paul: "It happens that our sepulchral life is interrupted by mysterious visits. At night, silently open the gates to the garden, leading to the common corridor which encircles the entire bastion on the inside. Someone walking with rapid steps, accompanied by servants and gendarmes, approaches one of the cells and remains there for an hour or two. Is it perhaps a bearer of comfort? No, here there is no place for goodness, here roam jackals and hyenas. Here appears the representative of a familiar institution, Mr. Sudeikin . . ."[34]

As a rule, Sudeikin tried to win over his prisoners by being friendly and courteous, acting as an equal and conveying the impression that he shared their concerns. Occasionally, however, he resorted to intimidation. This was his treatment of Ivan Okladskii, who had been arrested in July 1880 and tried in October of that year for attempting to blow up a tsarist train. At the trial, Okladskii behaved in an impudent manner, and in his closing statement declared: "I neither ask nor need to have my lot mitigated; on the contrary, were the court to moderate my sentence, I will consider it an insult."[35] Confronted with such defiance, Sudeikin resorted to browbeating. As Okladskii recalled:

> Sudeikin greeted me very severely and said that he knew me and had seen me previously. . . . Then he demanded that I tell him what went on outside, what other terrible plans the terrorist party had in mind, the party in which, according to him, I occu-

pied not the last place. I objected that I had no way of knowing that, being immured in the walls of the [Peter-Paul] fortress, cut off from everything alive among the free, and that I was merely a rank-and-file party worker who knew only that work in which I myself participated. After my response, he shouted in white fury that he will stop at nothing to extract from me some information, and that I should not forget I was now a convict without any rights with whom he could do whatever he wanted, and that he would not let me out of his hands until I submitted to his will. Then he shouted some more about his boundless power over all the prisons and convicted political criminals.[36]

The method worked, because Okladskii, for all his bravado in the courtroom, the very next year asked for pardon. This was granted, and after his release, he became a regular police informant, for which he was rewarded with hereditary burgher status and a pension. It was through his collaboration that the police apprehended most of the terrorists involved in the March 1, 1881, assassination of Alexander II.[*]

But Sudeikin much preferred to employ kindness and understanding. His objective was to persuade the jailed revolu-

---

[*] Kucharzewski, *Od bialego caratu*, 22–26. Although living under a changed name, he was arrested by the Soviet police in Petrograd in January 1924 and sentenced to death. Ibid., 26. The death sentence was commuted to ten years' imprisonment. N. A. Troitskii, *"Narodnaia volia" pered tsarskim sudom* (Saratov, 1983), 171.

tionaries that their activities not only did not advance the cause of freedom but had the opposite effect, strengthening the forces of reaction. He would propose instead a partnership between revolutionary youth and progressive elements in government, among which he included himself, jointly to struggle for the good of their country.

We possess several firsthand accounts of his procedures. One of his victims was P. S. Ivanovskaia, a founding member of the Executive Committee of the People's Will, arrested in 1882. Brought to his office, she had a good opportunity to observe him at work:

> Tall, athletically built, broad-shouldered, with the neck of a large ox, handsome face, lively black eyes, the very free and easy manners of a dyed-in-the-wool sergeant-major, his combined features resembled those of a well-fed and well-groomed stallion. . . . His speech flowed like a rapid stream, jumping from one subject to another without any connection. From the lips of the gendarme fell the names of great men, men of genius. Mentioned were K. Marx, Maudsley, Darwin, and, finally, Lombroso. He cited the latter to affirm the truth that everyone is possessed by madness, that there are no righteous and guilty people.[37]

Another witness is P. Ia. Osmolovskaia, an eighteen-year-old provincial girl, then in the eighth month of pregnancy, whom Sudeikin interrogated in the House of Preliminary Detention. She describes Sudeikin as a thick-set man with a lively face and rapid motions: his piercing eyes glistened like knives.

At the outset Sudeikin tried to put her at ease by saying that like her, he came from Smolensk. Then he engaged her in small talk, chatting about matters that had nothing to do with her case. He gradually shifted to politics, speaking more in sorrow than anger about the young people who got caught up in the revolutionary movement hoping to benefit their country only to perish without doing anyone any good. How much more would they accomplish if they only waited until they had matured and had a chance to think things over! He declared himself a constitutionalist who opposed terrorism because it thwarted reforms.

At one point he confided that he was seeking collaborators. Osmolovskaia interpreted these words as an invitation to spy on her comrades and indignantly refused.

"No, not at all!" Sudeikin responded. "This has nothing to do with spying, why take it this way? . . . I have no need of spies, detectives: I have as many of them as I need, at any price. I need people with *ideas* from the ranks of that honest youth which now joins the revolution [and] perishes uselessly for the sake of the fatherland. I need these people not for purposes of investigation—that is a job for hired spies—but to spread antirevolutionary propaganda among the young and to thwart terrorist designs."[38]

In 1882 the police arrested one Grebencho, a radical student who had been expelled from the University of St. Petersburg for taking part in a demonstration and subsequently jailed on suspicion of involvement in terrorist activities. In prison he was visited by Sudeikin, who outlined to him a whole program of economic reforms involving increases of peasant allotments and other measures to improve the lot of the common people. This program, Sudeikin assured him, enjoyed the support of influential persons within government or with close connections to it. It was terrorism that impeded it. He asked Grebencho to help promote change by joining the revolutionary underground and informing him of projected terrorist outrages in order to enable the police to thwart them. He assured Grebencho, as he had Osmolovskaia, that he was not expected to betray any of his comrades. Such betrayals were unnecessary because he, Sudeikin, was excellently informed about who was who and who did what in revolutionary ranks: to prove his point, he showed Grebencho a full and accurate list of all his meetings with fellow revolutionaries. Grebencho never carried out his promise to collaborate because he promptly fell into a severe depression and had to be committed to a psychiatric ward.[39]

To what lengths Sudeikin went to conceal his movements can be illustrated by his encounters with Grebencho after the latter had been released from prison. "I was told to come to a private apartment in a house on Bol'shaia Morskaia street, and when asked who I was, to give my name as Khalturin," Grebencho recalled.

> When I did so, I was led into an ordinary modest and small apartment and asked to wait. After a quarter of an hour, an individual showed up and asked me to follow him. On the street, he went ahead and I was to go behind him at a distance of approximately 100 steps. It turned out that at a similar distance behind me walked another police agent. The one in front, having come to Nevskii Prospekt, turned right and proceeded in the direction of the Kazan

cathedral. On reaching Kazan Street, he turned into Kazan square and crossed it in the direction of the Catherine Canal where stood a cab rank. Walking up to one of the cabs, he knocked on the door. The door opened and, as by this time I had drawn near, he asked me to enter. Inside sat Sudeikin. We left and traveled a fairly long time along many different streets. In the meantime it had grown dark, and Sudeikin released me from the cab on one of the secluded streets on the Petersburg side having slowed down its pace but without bringing it to a full stop.

Before parting, Sudeikin stuffed some money in the pocket of Grebencho's overcoat and made arrangements for another meeting.[40]

By such methods, Sudeikin managed to win over a number of revolutionaries, some of whom became regular spies, others who collaborated with him only until they concluded that he had deceived them. Among such collaborators was Vladimir Degaev, Sergei's younger brother.

Vladimir was seventeen years old when arrested in the fall of 1881 for distributing seditious literature. Like the rest of his family, he dreamed of fame and glory. He had made contacts with radical youths while a student at the Naval Academy: when the authorities became aware of these links, they expelled him.

Everyone who knew Vladimir Degaev at that time described him in glowing terms as a charming, idealistic youth.

Vladimir Degaev

Vera Figner recalled him fondly as a "good, gentle" lad who would importune her to tell him when the revolution would at last break out—in three months? or perhaps six?—and showed keen disappointment when she responded this was something no one could predict.[41] A. P. Pribyleva-Korba, like Figner a member of the Executive Committee, also spoke of his "childishly pure" soul and passionate belief in the coming revolution.[42]

In prison, Vladimir was interrogated by Sudeikin, who

described himself as a progressive and to prove it produced a copy of Marx's *Capital.* He said that the government desired peace with the revolutionaries in order to carry out a comprehensive program of reforms. The revolutionaries prevented the implementation of this program, Sudeikin said, asking Vladimir to persuade his friends to refrain from terrorism.[43] But he also hinted that he would welcome a long-term relationship with him, for, aware as he was of his family's revolutionary sympathies and connections, he intended, with his help, to penetrate the terrorist underground. Vladimir responded that he needed time to consider the offer but that under no circumstances would he betray anyone. This sufficed for Sudeikin, who ordered him released from prison.

On regaining his freedom, Vladimir told Sergei what had transpired. Sergei, in turn, contacted Savelii Solomonovich Zlatopolskii, the sole member of the Executive Committee then in St. Petersburg. Acting on his own authority, Zlatopolskii advised Vladimir to accept Sudeikin's offer. To illuminate this puzzling decision it is necessary to say a few words about the situation of the People's Will at the time.

Just as Sudeikin was desperate to penetrate the revolutionary ranks, so were the revolutionaries desperate to infiltrate his headquarters. They had become aware of Sudeikin's tactics and feared that if unchecked he would destroy what was left of their organization. To stop him, they needed to subvert his formidable police apparatus from within by planting an agent inside the St. Petersburg gendarme headquarters. Such a person would expose police spies in their ranks as well as track the elusive gendarme's movements in order to enable the revolutionaries to assassinate him.

This was not as impossible a goal as might seem, for they had had such a spy a short time before in the person of Nikolai Vasilevich Kletochnikov.[44] A justice of the peace and later a member of the People's Will, in the winter of 1878–79 Kletochnikov, with the approval of his colleagues, found employment with the Third Department. (He had been recommended by his landlady, an elderly woman whom he had managed to charm.) He worked so efficiently for the police that they entrusted him with ever greater responsibilities and eventually gave him access to the most secret information regarding the struggle with the revolutionary underground. All this time, he informed the People's Will about police activities, including who was placed under surveillance.[45] The knowledge he imparted of police agents proved invaluable: he is estimated to have revealed the identity of more than three hundred spies.[46] The revolutionaries credited him with their ability throughout 1879 and 1880 to elude the police and develop an effective organization.[47] Unfortunately for them, Kletochnikov was unmasked in January 1881. Sentenced to death in the so-called Trial of Twenty a year later, he had his sentence commuted by the tsar to lifelong hard labor, which he served in the Alekseev Bastion of the Peter-Paul fortress. He died there in July 1883 following a hunger strike.

Sudeikin's offer to Vladimir Degaev seemed to Zlatopolskii to present an unexpected opportunity to plant another agent in the enemy camp, and he seized it, even though the circumstances were quite different, in that Kletochnikov had been a trusted government employee who could serve the revolutionaries without betraying anyone, whereas Vladimir, in order to gain the trust of the police, had no choice but to turn revolutionaries over to it. The young man's head reeled with excitement at the thought that he would replicate the famous deeds of Kletochnikov: he came to believe himself chosen by destiny to play this historic role.[48]

As it turned out, the inexperienced Vladimir Degaev would perform greater services for Sudeikin than for the revolutionaries. Unversed in conspiratorial ways, he made it possible for police agents to shadow him and thus to identify and establish the whereabouts of the leading figures of the organization.

In December 1881 Vladimir asked Sudeikin for permission and funds to go abroad to investigate the revolutionary emigration.[49] On arriving in Geneva he contacted Lev Deich, an associate of the Marxist Liberation of Labor Group, to whom he proudly introduced himself as the "new Kletochnikov." Deich took one look at the visitor, who struck him as a mere boy, and burst into laughter.[50] From Geneva, Vladimir proceeded to Paris, but he met everywhere with a cool reception, for Zlatopolskii had forewarned the émigrés by letter that Vladimir was in Sudeikin's employ. He came back empty-handed, and Sudeikin began to wonder whether he had made a wise investment. He eventually dismissed him and, saying that he did not want ever again to hear from or about him, ordered him to volunteer for military service in Saratov.

While this was happening, the revolutionary organization underwent changes. Zlatopolskii was arrested in Moscow in March; he was replaced in St. Petersburg by another member of the Executive Committee, Mikhail Fedorovich Grachevskii. Grachevskii decided that Sudeikin had to go. In utmost secrecy,

M. F. Grachevskii

he set up a dynamite laboratory in the apartment of Alexander Pribylev and his wife, Rose.

To succeed, it was essential to track Sudeikin's movements, and to this end Grachevskii requested that Sergei Degaev make contact with the gendarme. He instructed Vladimir to tell Sudeikin that his elder brother needed work, which

Vladimir did before leaving for Saratov. Sudeikin invited Sergei for an interview in a wooden hut in the suburbs of St. Petersburg.[51] Informed that Sergei was a skilled draftsman, Sudeikin offered him a job designing blueprints for a projected police building. The two men met subsequently several times to discuss Sergei's assignment. The encounters yielded no information useful to Grachevskii, and in April 1882 Sergei Degaev broke off contacts with Sudeikin, following which he departed for the Caucasus; his wife joined him in July. According to her, they had left St. Petersburg because Sergei thought that he was being shadowed. At the same time, Sudeikin, who trusted no one, had Sergei's sister, Natalie, placed under surveillance.[52]

Grachevskii now devised a plan which involved Osmolovskaia, whom, as we have seen, Sudeikin hoped to engage in his service. She was to carry around her neck a bomb which she would explode while in his office. For some reason—possibly because Sudeikin had gotten wind of it—the plan fell through. Sudeikin, well informed of Grachevskii's movements from Vladimir's incautious encounters with the People's Will, on the night of June 4–5 arrested Grachevskii along with 120 associates, decapitating in one fell swoop the entire revolutionary cadre in the capital city.[53] Alexander III was delighted with the news, all the more because the bombs that Grachevskii's dynamite laboratory was producing might have been meant for him.* For this brilliant coup, the tsar awarded Sudeikin 15,000

* Indeed, later that year, in a letter to General P. V. Orzhevskii, his immediate superior, Sudeikin presented the aborted terrorist act of Grachevskii's as intended against the tsar: GARF, Fond 102, 3 DP, 1882, delo 782, list 4.

rubles.* Two weeks later, on June 18, Sudeikin received promotion to the rank of lieutenant colonel.

After these arrests, Tikhomirov and Maria Oshanina, also a member of the Executive Committee, both of whom had eluded capture, decided not to tempt fate further and fled to the West. This left Vera Figner as the sole member of the committee still at liberty: she firmly refused to emigrate and took up residence under false papers in Kharkov. The center of the People's Will now shifted to the south, the Ukraine and the Caucasus.

Having left town two months before the June raid, Sergei Degaev also was not affected by it. He spent the summer of 1882 with his wife in Georgia, working for a company which was constructing a railway linking Tiflis and Baku. His reputation as an intrepid revolutionary preceded him, and local radicals received him warmly. Speaking in the name of the Executive Committee—which he had no right to do—he demanded complete subordination to his orders. The revolutionaries were to gather information on local military units and recruit from among them fresh members. To obtain money, Degaev devised a plan to rob the Gori branch of the treasury by intoxicating the guards, but it fell through.[54]†

In September 1882, on instructions of Vera Figner, the Degaevs left Tiflis for Kharkov. Figner was now the effective

---

* F[eliks] Lure, *Politseiskie i provokatory* (St. Petersburg, 1992), 209. Grachevskii was sentenced in the so-called Trial of Seventeen to capital punishment but the sentence was commuted to lifelong confinement in the Schlüsselburg Fortress. There in 1887 he poured kerosene over himself, set it on fire, and burned to death.

† Gori, at this time, was the home of the two-year-old Stalin.

leader of what was left of the People's Will. Her strategy was
to counter Sudeikin's measures by creating throughout the empire many small independent groups of ten to twenty members
each that were to follow directives of the Executive Committee but avoid communicating with one another so as to prevent
police infiltration. Terror was to continue: its first victim was
to be Sudeikin himself, to be followed by the minister of the
interior, Dmitrii Tolstoy.[55]

Figner asked Degaev to contact People's Will sympathizers in the military, and with this intention he traveled to St.
Petersburg.[56] The officers held him in the highest esteem: one
of them goes so far as to say they "worshiped" him as "subtle,
adroit, wise, wily, and enterprising."[57] Even so, he came back
discouraged: neither at the Kronshtadt naval base nor in nearby
St. Petersburg did he find much revolutionary fervor.[58] He re-
luctantly concluded that there simply were not adequate forces
in the capital to revive terrorism.[59] Sudeikin's mass arrests of the
previous June, it turned out, had all but destroyed the northern
branch of the People's Will.

Figner now instructed Degaev to move to Odessa to set
up a secret printing press that would publish no. 10 of the
party's theoretical organ, *Narodnaia Volia*, the last number of
which had appeared in February 1882. The equipment was to be
secretly transported from Moscow, where it had fortuitously escaped seizure.[60] Degaev followed her directions and on November 16 moved to Odessa. In early December, using passports
made out in the name of a Lieutenant Suvorov, he and his
wife rented a five-room apartment with kitchen, on Uspenskii
Pereulok 8, apartment 27.[61] Assisting them was Mariia Kaliuzhnaia, a sixteen-year-old merchant's daughter posing as a ser-

Mariia Kaliuzhnaia

vant.[62] Dmitrii Surovtsev, another collaborator and a veteran revolutionary, who had fled from exile four years earlier and since then led an illegal existence, took quarters in another part of town.[63] Both had been assigned by Figner.

On December 8, 1882, the police placed the Degaev residence under surveillance. The following day, a police agent observed Surovtsev transporting a large suitcase and a wicker basket from the railroad terminal to the Degaevs' apartment. A week later, the Degaevs were joined by the twenty-eight-year-old A. A. Spandoni-Basmandzhi, who had been assigned by Figner to maintain contact between the Odessa press and the "outside world"—to bring in materials for publication and to distribute its output.[64] Spandoni, the son of a Greek merchant from Odessa, had been arrested in 1878 and exiled to Siberia. He was allowed in 1881 to return to European Russia but kept under police surveillance. He brought news from Vera Figner that she had dispatched to Odessa several hundred pounds of type, one part meant for the Degaevs, another for his own press.

According to Degaev, he soon attracted police attention. While the printing press was being set up, Degaev frequented the Odessa Public Library in order to lull suspicions of neighbors. But Figner, he said, oblivious of his precautions, "dispatched to Odessa to maintain relations with Degaev" Spandoni, "who had been previously arrested there and was known to all of Odessa's detectives and gendarmes." On his arrival, Spandoni "approached Degaev in broad daylight on the street, as the latter left the library. This was observed by the detective who for a long time had been following Spandoni. The detective trailed Degaev, who was arrested. . . . Such extraordinary carelessness proved to Degaev that Figner either attached no value whatever to the lives of her friends or else was incapable of choosing people."[65] Degaev said that this event, which occurred on December 18, was the principal reason why he turned against Figner and the organization which she directed.

In fact, Degaev's version of his arrest is a lie, designed to justify his betrayal of Figner. First, his apartment had come under surveillance ten days before Spandoni arrived in Odessa.

A. A. Spandoni

Second, according to Degaev's wife, who spoke freely to the gendarmes following her arrest, Spandoni customarily met her husband on the street and visited their apartment only twice.[66]

The search of the Degaev apartment revealed a fully equipped printing press as well as many photographs of official personalities, forged visas, and revolutionary publications.[67] Degaev refused to give the police any information apart from his true name, which should put to rest suspicions, voiced by some historians, that he had turned into a police agent during his 1881 arrest.*

Degaev found himself in prison for the second time in his life. The prospects now were far more dismal than a year and a half earlier, when he had been released for lack of evidence. Now he had been caught red-handed setting up an illegal press to print revolutionary material. The tsarist government viewed such activity to be only slightly less serious than acts of terrorism. Suffice it to say that Degaev's associate, Spandoni, arrested on January 10, 1883, on the same charges, would be sentenced to fifteen years of hard labor. Some revolutionaries faced this prospect with equanimity, but Degaev was not one of them: he valued his life and freedom.

There is no evidence that would allow us to determine what went through his mind as he sat in his cell at the Odessa prison. Degaev many years later tried to write his memoirs, but, as he confessed to his brother, nothing came of it.[68] The Polish historian Jan Kucharzewski speculates that "restless ambition and the instinct of self-preservation rebel[led] against the somber prospect of a broken life."[69] Which factor predominated cannot, of course, be ascertained. But it seems clear from the rapidity with which he acted that the idea of collaborating with the authorities must have been germinating in his mind for some time.

In letters which Degaev sent his brother Vladimir a quar-

---

* F[eliks] Lure, *Politseiskie i provokatory* (St. Petersburg, 1992), 176, believes that Degaev became an agent of Sudeikin's already in May 1882. In this he follows Lev Deich, *Provokatory i terror* (Tula, 1926), 21–22.

ter of a century later to justify his past behavior, he claimed
that he had concluded that the People's Will was finished. He
placed much of the blame for its demise on Vera Figner, who, in
his judgment, refused to face reality and carried on in a manner that only caused young men like himself to end up behind
bars if not on the gallows: "Contrary to all dictates of common
sense and reality, Figner continued to conduct the affairs of the
People's Will, having neither the personnel nor the talents to
direct this work, the result of which was Sudeikin's infiltration
and playing at revolution, which was followed by numerous
arrests without any benefit to the party."[70] The arrests of the
Grachevskii circle in St. Petersburg (for which Vera Figner bore
no blame) and the flight abroad of Tikhomirov and Oshanina
convinced Degaev that the old party had no future.[71] Indeed,
since Sudeikin had taken charge of security affairs in the capital a year and a half earlier, terrorism had virtually ceased. The
revolutionaries could not even manage to install a secret printing press. The loss of the Odessa press was a disaster. It was a
matter of the greatest importance for the People's Will to distribute its publications in order to demonstrate to the public at
large as well as to the government that despite the massive arrests and the absence of terrorist activities, the party was alive.
Goldenberg had broken down when he learned that one of the
People's Will's presses had been seized: "To deprive us of an
organ," he wrote in his "Confession," "means to deprive us of
our soul, it means to suffer defeat."[72]

Vera Figner, too, thought that with the discovery of the
Odessa press the last chance to publish a clandestine party
organ had vanished. She concluded that all her efforts, under-
taken at such great personal risk, had been in vain.[73] At least

one historian agrees that with the Odessa arrests in December 1882 "began the de facto liquidation of the People's Will."[74] Degaev later told Tikhomirov that he had been "crushed" by the loss of the press: of the People's Will leaders, only Vera Figner was still at liberty, and she was incompetent; the others were worse than useless.[75]

What was to be done? Because the old ways were clearly no longer feasible, one either had to abandon the struggle altogether or try something drastically new. If there were progressive people in the government, why not cooperate with them? Why not exploit divisions in the enemy camp instead of treating it as a hostile monolith? The thoughts that crossed Degaev's mind were not unlike those that had persuaded Goldenberg three years earlier to cooperate with the police authorities, with that difference that Degaev was inspired less by dread of interminable murders and executions than by the feeling that rather than fight the government in order to change Russia for the better one ought to collaborate with it. Degaev's elder sister, Natalie, drops a significant hint when she writes, in her recollections of conversations with him both in Russia and in emigration, that he had hoped to achieve revolutionary goals through the government.[76]

Degaev could well recall the conversations that Vladimir had had with Sudeikin earlier in the year in which the gendarme had pleaded for cooperation with antiterrorist radicals.

Refusing to talk to the Odessa gendarmes, Degaev wrote a letter which he asked them to forward to Sudeikin in St. Petersburg expressing a desire to see him. Sudeikin wasted no time responding, and on the eve of Christmas left for Odessa to hear what Degaev had to say.

CHAPTER FOUR

The Police Run the Revolution

When he received Degaev's letter, Sudeikin, too, was in the midst of a personal crisis.

He had been for a long time irritated that his work was hindered by interference from other government agencies, which aborted his carefully laid plans by arresting revolutionaries whom he had placed under surveillance. This was largely the result of a division of labor between the police and the gendarmerie established in 1871 by virtue of which the former tracked and arrested political criminals, while the latter interrogated them and prepared formal depositions eliciting admissions of guilt. Sudeikin wanted complete control over the struggle against sedition: and unless he could obtain it, he was prepared to withdraw into private life. On October 25, 1882, he addressed an angry letter to his immediate superior, Deputy Interior Minister General P. V. Orzhevskii, in which, complaining of one such incident of interference, he requested that

> the higher authorities resolve the principal question: what ought to take precedence in the struggle against sedition—a formal inquest, whose purpose it is to establish the guilt of criminals who have already committed the crime, or the secret service, whose task, in my judgment, it is to prevent this crime? . . . For the time being I will confine myself to expressing the generally known truth that formal inquest has existed since 1871 and exists to this day, yet sedition has not yielded to its pressure, evolving ever more [and] exploding in the crime of March 1 [1881]. Formal inquest has failed to prevent a single crime. The secret service, where it has really operated, notwithstanding its relatively short existence, has accomplished more. But it can function successfully only if formal inquest collaborates with it.[1]

To add force to his complaint, Sudeikin ended the letter by submitting his resignation.

The letter was forwarded to the police. That department acknowledged that Sudeikin was right but observed that the underlying problem of division of authority was long entrenched.[2] Sudeikin managed, however, to clear this obstacle. On December 3, 1882, he was promoted to the post of inspector of the secret police for the conduct of political investigation—a position especially created for him and abolished after his death. Its creation was not publicized at the time.[3] It gave him control over the St. Petersburg and Moscow secret police bureaus as well as the investigative sections of the gendarme administrations of Moscow, Kharkov, Kiev, and Kherson provinces and the city of Odessa, the principal centers of revolutionary activity in the empire. Other branches of the government involved in the fight against sedition in these localities were to undertake no moves without his sanction.[4] He was thus placed in charge of protecting the tsarist regime from subversion: a sign of extraordinary confidence in his abilities and the basis of enormous power. At the age of thirty-three, he had attained the pinnacle of a police career.

And yet, although his demands had been met and his powers greatly enhanced, he was an unhappy and frustrated man. He had a jaundiced view of tsarist Russia: he regarded those whom he served as hopeless incompetents. Once, in an expansive mood, he told a prisoner: "At the head of Russia's progress . . . today advance the revolutionaries and gendarmes. They ride at a trot. Behind them follow on post chaises the liberals. Ordinary citizens drag slowly and the rear is brought up on foot by peasants, covered with gray dust, wiping the sweat off their faces and paying all the travel costs."[5] Such subversive opinions, which depicted the gendarmes as partners of the revolutionaries, were, of course, intended to gain the confidence of those revolutionaries whom Sudeikin hoped to involve in his schemes. But he also harbored a genuine—and not unjustified—grudge against the tsarist establishment which he served with outstanding efficiency but which rewarded him in a most niggardly manner. As he often confided to Degaev after they had gotten to know each other better, "He was dissatisfied by the disparity between the insignificance of his position in the [official] hierarchy and his real significance as the protector of the reigning person, and the order and peace in the capital and the Empire."[6]

In June 1882 he had been promoted to lieutenant colonel, which conferred on him the rather lowly seventh level on the Table of Ranks, the charter which since the days of Peter the Great had determined status in the armed forces as well as the civil service. This made him ineligible to have an audience with the tsar, who, by tradition, did not receive officials below level four.[7] Yet Sudeikin dreamed of such an audience, convinced that "the man who could control Russian terrorism would stand closest to the tsar."[8] If only he met the tsar face to face once, he felt, he could exert enormous influence on him and make himself indispensable.[9]

To make matters still worse, in spite of the important post he held and the grave responsibilities he carried, he was cold-shouldered by the bureaucratic establishment as well as St. Petersburg society. In the words of Tikhomirov, Sudeikin's plebeian background and his inferior education, combined with his not very reputable duties (and, one might add, the kind of clandestine existence he had to lead), estranged him from those who molded opinion in the capital city: "His ignorance, not disguised by any social polish, his barrack-like manners, and, finally the very nature of the service which brought him renown, all this shocked the upper circles and made them reject with revulsion the thought that this man could ever become a 'somebody.'"[10] The aristocratic minister of the interior, Count Dmitrii Tolstoy, in particular, treated Sudeikin disdainfully, for which Sudeikin repaid him with loathing.

There were other factors as well working against him. Tolstoy and the minister of police, Viacheslav Plehve, blocked his advancement for fear of jeopardizing their own positions: they could not fail to sense his aspiration to replace them. As his future actions indicated, Sudeikin himself lay the blame at their door. Plehve assured Sudeikin that next to the tsar's no life was as important to Russia as his, and yet he was not promoted to general and could not contrive a meeting with the tsar whose life he was protecting.[11] The authorities may also have regarded him as youthfully "exuberant" and overly independent, not quite a "team player."[12] Whatever the reason for his treatment, he resented it, and in time his resentment turned into an obsession: it caused him to despise the regime as much as did the revolutionaries. It gave him no peace and led him to concoct a fantastic conspiracy against his superiors, which would, he believed, through the workings of a revolutionary plot under his personal control, finally bring him the rewards he deserved. To carry it out, he needed a revolutionary ally. He found him in Degaev.

A Polish historian of the Russian revolutionary movement speculates that Sudeikin sensed, as did the Executive Committee, that Degaev was not a committed revolutionary but rather someone who sought in the revolutionary movement the fulfillment of personal aspirations. On this basis, the theory goes, Sudeikin proposed to him an alliance.[13] Degaev had his own grievances which made him responsive to Sudeikin's advances. Their collaboration thus turned into a partnership of thwarted ambitions.

As we have seen, despite his services to the People's Will since 1880, Degaev had been refused admittance to its Executive

Committee on the grounds that he was insufficiently "revolutionary." A naval officer acquainted with Degaev confirms this impression. Although Degaev was loyal to the People's Will, the officer writes, and was loved by many of its members, he did not inspire confidence: his "devotion to the cause and the party was only intellectual, while his heart, even if it participated, did so to a very limited extent: it was involuntarily felt that he was an *associate,* not a *comrade.*"[14] Another revolutionary described him as "endowed with a weak character, vain, strongly attached to his life, with very poorly developed moral convictions."[15] And we have cited the opinion of Vera Figner that he lacked originality and displayed softness and submissiveness—qualities suitable for a follower, not a leader. This was not a role he envisaged for himself. It rankled.

Degaev contributed to his reputation by revealing an aversion to murder. He further confessed a dread of execution, especially by hanging.[16] In circles in which taking life and sacrificing one's own life were considered matters of little consequence, the unwillingness to kill another human being betokened "weakness" and disqualified him from membership in the party's directing organ.

Our information on what transpired between Degaev and Sudeikin in the Odessa prison in late December 1882 derives from two sources: the recollections of Degaev's elder sister, Natalie, published in 1906,[17] and the memoirs of Lev Tikhomirov, based on what Degaev had told him in early 1884 but which he committed to paper only forty years after the event.[18] The problem with both accounts is that they conflate the chronology, making it appear as if the relationship between Degaev and Sudeikin immediately assumed confidential terms, whereas in reality the relationship evolved over months.

Natalie Degaev-Makletsova met her brother secretly in the antechamber to a Kharkov bathhouse some time late in 1883, at which time he revealed to her his relationship with Sudeikin. He told her that Sudeikin had impressed him as being more of a revolutionary than a gendarme because he spoke with such contempt of Russia's rulers and agreed that the country needed fundamental change. The revolutionaries, Sudeikin told him, were struggling for such change but employed the wrong methods. He went on to persuade Degaev that continuing to work for the People's Will would cost him his life and yet serve no purpose.

So far, this was typical Sudeikin, the line he had taken with other imprisoned revolutionaries. But on this occasion he is said to have gone much further, unfolding a fantastic scheme of collaboration between the police and the terrorists that in its audacity had neither precedent nor sequel in Russian history. Treating Degaev as a leading figure in what was left of the People's Will, Sudeikin proposed an alliance in which Degaev, under Sudeikin's secret patronage and acting on his orders, would direct terrorist assaults against high government officials, which would frighten the government into making major reforms.

This account, though given both by Degaev's sister and by Tikhomirov, cannot be taken at face value. It is inconceivable that a seasoned police official like Sudeikin would instantly confide to an arrested revolutionary, whom he scarcely knew, a plot against the government — a plot which, if the revolutionary chose to reveal it to the authorities, would lead to Sudeikin's immediate arrest on charges of high treason. Sudeikin did make such a proposal, but it came later, in the course of the summer, after he had become friendly with Degaev and when his rage against the government had reached high pitch.

It is far more likely that during this, their first encounter, Sudeikin proposed to his prisoner limited collaboration. Degaev would help the authorities disarm the terrorist underground, in return for which Sudeikin would enable him to assume the leadership of a radical party committed to non-violence. Sudeikin would introduce Degaev to the tsar, and forces would be set in motion that would lead Russia peacefully toward reform. Of course, in his new role Degaev would have to betray his comrades, who would end up in jail. But did not the revolutionary ethic dictate that the end justified the means? Degaev rationalized this prospect by thinking of himself as a general who orders into combat the troops entrusted to his command, though aware that he was sending many of them to their death. In September 1884 the official journal of the People's Will Party published a brief account of Degaev's past. According to the account, Degaev said that when he had struck his deal with Sudeikin, he believed that he would be required to turn over only revolutionaries of the second rank, and that only under relentless police pressure was he forced to betray nearly all.[19]

Having heard out Sudeikin's offer, Degaev said that he wished to consult his wife, who was also imprisoned. A meeting was promptly arranged. She recalled the following scene: "Seryozha is sitting with Sudeikin. On the table stand a bottle of wine and pirogi. 'Sit down, Liubochka, have some pirogi,' Degaev said. 'Don't you want wine?'"[20] A simple woman with unshakable faith in her husband, she agreed to whatever he wanted. Half a year later, Degaev told Tikhomirov that having made the decision to collaborate with Sudeikin, he and his wife experienced in prison deliriously happy moments: "Amid these sweet and festive sensations they celebrated the [Christmas] holiday with tasty dishes and drinks, dreaming of the great deeds which Degaev would perform in the future. During those minutes, he experienced such luminous feelings that even now he recalled them with deep emotion, painting an almost artistic picture: the dark, destitute surroundings of the prison cell, barely illuminated by a dim lamp, on the one hand, and on the other two human spirits, illuminated by the bright lights of joy and exultation."[21] Like Goldenberg three years earlier, Degaev felt it was the happiest moment of his life, opening up dizzying prospects for the cause as well as for himself personally.

During the next two weeks, he supplied the police with the names and addresses of all the members of the People's Will of whom he had knowledge.[22] For the major part they were young officers, members of the military branch with which he had close connections. Degaev further provided detailed lists of individuals who showed sympathy for the party and could be expected, at any time, to join its ranks. But he also revealed the whereabouts of Vera Figner, whom the authorities rightly regarded as the linchpin of what remained of the terrorist organization: until she was behind bars, Degaev could not play the role to which he aspired and which Sudeikin had in mind for him, that of an unchallenged leader of the reconstructed—and thoroughly tamed—People's Will. For the time being, the persons whom he had fingered were left at liberty, for Sudeikin did not want to arouse suspicions that Degaev had exposed them. The arrests were carried out only in February and March.*

In order for Degaev to carry out the work for which Sudeikin had designated him, he had somehow to be set free. Sudeikin, never at a loss for solutions, contrived in utmost secrecy to arrange his escape. To still suspicions, Spandoni, who had been jailed in Odessa on January 10, was placed in a solitary cell adjoining Degaev's. On January 11 the two communicated by means of taps on the wall separating them. Degaev informed Spandoni that he had been involved in the assassination in Kiev of the gendarme G. E. Geiking, whose killer had never been apprehended. This surprised Spandoni, for the murder had taken place five years earlier. He further apprised Spandoni that the authorities regarded him as an agent of the Executive Committee and that, as such, he faced capital punishment. He had to contrive some way of escaping, and he thought that he had his best chance in Kiev.[23] These lies served to justify Degaev's transfer from Odessa to Kiev, agreed upon with Sudeikin, during which he would stage his "escape."

Around 7:00 P.M. on January 14, 1883, while being escorted by two noncommissioned gendarme officers in an open carriage to the Odessa railway terminal for the trip to Kiev, Degaev tore loose. He pushed one gendarme out of the carriage into the snow and threw tobacco in the other's face, tempo-

---

*Degaev's list is in GARF, Fond 102, 3 DP, 1884, delo 208. See also Figner, *Trud,* 368–69. The most important of those named by Degaev, headed by Figner, were tried in September 1884 in the so-called Trial of Fourteen. Among them were Spandoni and Surovtsev. Ibid., 433.

rarily blinding him. He then dashed into the railroad building, then still under construction. Two shots missed him. A search party equipped with lanterns failed to locate any trace of him. He had simply vanished. It seems that the Odessa gendarmes had collaborated with this charade.* Later that day, Lieutenant Colonel Katanskii sent to St. Petersburg a terse telegram: "State criminal Sergei Degaev escaped this evening."[24]

Degaev contacted an army officer connected with the People's Will who offered him temporary shelter and then arranged to get him to Nikolaev, where he hid out for a few days with the family of another officer. From there he made his way to Kharkov. On January 23 or 24, Vera Figner was invited to visit friends: there, to her great surprise, she encountered Degaev.[25] Like everyone else, she was delighted with his miraculous escape. She was surprised, however, to find him gloomy and restless: she explained this mood to herself as worry over his wife, whom he had left behind in prison. To deflect suspicion from himself before the police, acting on his information, began to round up revolutionaries, Degaev let it be known that someone in Odessa was squealing.[26]

According to Vera Figner, not long after this meeting Degaev visited her in the apartment where she lived under an assumed name as a student in a local school for midwives. When he casually asked her when she left her house in the morning, she told him that it was around 8. A few days later, on Febru-

---

* "Nezavisimyi," *Utro Rossii,* April 1913. A document in GARF, Fond 102, o.o., 1902 g., d. 624, citing a gendarme by the name of Porfirii Volkov, states that the two gendarmes "enjoyed the confidence of Sudeikin."

ary 10 at 8:00 A.M., immediately after Figner had left home, she ran into Vasily Merkulov, a worker who had once belonged to the People's Will but whom in April 1881 Sudeikin had managed to turn into a police agent. Merkulov knew Vera Figner personally and was brought from St. Petersburg to Kharkov to identify her in order to deflect suspicion from Degaev. Surrounded by gendarmes and escorted to the police station, she tried unsuccessfully to swallow an incriminating piece of paper. (She succeeded later.) The next day she was dispatched by train to St. Petersburg.*

Her capture represented yet another triumph for Sudeikin. The event was judged to be so important that both Sudeikin and Plehve came to Kharkov incognito to be on hand when it happened.[27] The tsar exulted upon learning that Figner was behind bars: "Thank God!" he wrote, "This terrible woman has been arrested!"† He had been informed by Tolstoy of the role Degaev played in her arrest.[28] The revolutionaries, for their part, were perplexed, for they had considered her quite safe.[29]

Guided by lists provided by Degaev,[30] the police now proceeded to round up some revolutionaries while placing others under surveillance. Following his leads, in March 1883 they arrested 140 officers with revolutionary connections. Many if not most readily confessed and asked forgiveness.[31] They received

---

* Figner, *Trud,* 359–60. *Obzor* 7 (July 1, 1883–January 1, 1884), 12, asserts that Degaev gave the police her address, but V. I. Chuiko in *Narodovol'tsy,* Sbornik III (Moscow, 1931), 185–86, claims that her apartment was not discovered and her papers not searched.

† Figner, *Trud,* 361. The following year, when the court sentenced Figner to death, Alexander III commuted the sentence to lifelong hard labor.

light sentences or were let go. This spelled the end of the military organization of the People's Will.[32] But Degaev rendered no less of a service to Sudeikin by revealing just how weak the People's Will really was after the arrests of 1881–82 and how limited its opportunities for causing harm.[33] This knowledge encouraged the government to give up attempts to come to terms with the radical opposition and to pursue instead an uncompromisingly repressive policy.[34]

Degaev in the meanwhile came under increased suspicion from his comrades. Some thought odd the circumstances of his escape. Why was he, a dangerous political criminal, escorted to the train by only two gendarmes? Where and how did he obtain the tobacco with which he had disabled one of his escorts, given that he did not smoke? Why was he not recaptured? Spandoni, who learned of the escape somewhat later, claimed immediately to have suspected foul play because political prisoners were not transported in such a casual manner and because Degaev could not have obtained tobacco in prison. Such doubts gained considerable currency when in March 1883 word got around that a certain colonel from Nikolaev, having had a bit too much to drink at a private dinner in Odessa, had revealed that Degaev's famous "escape" had been staged, and that acting on the information Degaev had supplied, the authorities in Nikolaev arrested the very officers who had concealed him.[35] This information was at once conveyed to both Paris and Kharkov: from Kharkov came an angry response accusing the writers of slandering a prominent revolutionary. But in the south suspicions of Degaev gained credence and never abated.

In May 1883 Sudeikin sent Degaev to Switzerland. An avid reader of adventure stories, Sudeikin was enchanted by the sequel to Alexander Dumas's *Three Musketeers,* a novel called *The Vicomte de Bragelone.* Featured in it was the historical figure of General George Monk, who played a prominent role in the restoration of the Stuarts to the English throne. In the Dumas story, Monk wants to succeed Cromwell and rejects overtures from the future Charles II. D'Artagnan, who, like his comrades, is a staunch royalist, undertakes to kidnap Monk and bring him to Holland, thus enabling Charles II to reconquer his kingdom. Disguised as a fisherman, D'Artagnan delivers Monk in a boat to the Netherlands, after which the kidnapped general enters the future king's service and helps to restore him to the throne.

Fascinated by this fiction, Sudeikin wanted Degaev similarly to seize and deliver to Germany two revolutionary émigrés, Tikhomirov and Peter Lavrov, the latter a prominent radical publicist with close ties to the People's Will. From there, Sudeikin was confident that he would be able to extradite them to Russia.[36]

Degaev played along with this fantasy, but in fact he had something else in mind. He wanted to sound out Tikhomirov, the titular leader of the People's Will, about his own double role and to reach some kind of understanding that would extricate him from his increasingly painful predicament.

Why did he take this fateful step? There are at least four possible explanations.

One is that he was troubled by his conscience. That is the explanation he gave to one of his colleagues, Vasily Karaulov.[37]

It seems unlikely, though, that barely four months after deciding to work for Sudeikin, Degaev would feel such remorse as to risk being killed by his comrades for treason.

Another explanation, provided by the St. Petersburg terrorist Pribyleva-Korba, is that Degaev resolved to confess because he had learned that the People's Will was about to convene a council to try him for alleged treachery.[38] Alas, there is no corroborating evidence for this claim.

A more plausible explanation is that Degaev came to realize that the bargain he had struck with Sudeikin was not what he had expected and that Sudeikin was using him to advance his own career. Their agreement called for Sudeikin to play a passive role in the revolutionary movement. Yet he had immediately intervened in its affairs and, in order to impress his superiors, arrested persons Degaev preferred to leave at liberty. Nor had Sudeikin, contrary to his promise, presented Degaev to the tsar (which, as we know and Degaev did not, he could not do, never having been presented to the tsar himself). At the meeting with his sister in the Kharkov bathhouse in late 1883, Degaev, referring to Sudeikin, said: "This scoundrel has utterly deceived me. He has not presented me to the tsar, he introduced me only to Tolstoy and Pobedonostsev. It seems he wants to turn me into a common spy. For this I will avenge myself."[39] Caught between Sudeikin's exploitation of him and the risk of revolutionary punishment, he chose to make a clean breast, in the hope that by explaining the political rationale behind his actions, he would save his reputation and even his very life.

Forty years later Tikhomirov provided still another explanation. At their encounter at Mornex, near Geneva, he and

Degaev had talked for several days.[40] Degaev had insisted that the situation of the People's Will organization in Russia had become hopeless and that it might make sense to consider co-operating with the government. Tikhomirov agreed with him to the point of speculating whether it would not be possible to reach some sort of a compromise with the authorities. These reflections may have suggested to Degaev that Tikhomirov might understand and condone his actions.[41] And so he blurted out: "Look . . . let us not play hide-and-seek. I will tell you frankly the whole truth, and then judge me. I am in your hands. Whatever you say, I will do."[42]

He then proceeded to describe how after his arrest the previous December and the seizure of his printing press, he had felt that the movement had no future unless it took a radically different tack. He had written to request a meeting with Sudeikin, who claimed to be a "populist." The two agreed to work in tandem, Sudeikin exerting pressure on the government, Degaev on the revolutionaries. So it happened that around Christmas 1882 he had turned into a police informant, revealing all that he knew about the revolutionary movement: names and aliases, addresses, and so on. At one point, while confessing to these betrayals, Degaev lowered his head and wondered aloud whether Sudeikin was not deceiving him.

What should he do? Tikhomirov answered that the revolutionaries could kill him for his treachery, but that it would be better if he first warned and saved those comrades in Russia who, because of his betrayals, were at risk of arrest. Then, Tikhomirov said, he should kill Sudeikin. Degaev's face brightened at this answer, and he agreed to Tikhomirov's suggestion.

Shortly after this dramatic encounter Tikhomirov left for

Paris to consult the other member of the Executive Committee in emigration, Maria Oshanina (Mariia N. Olovennikova; also known as Marina Polonskaia).

Afraid of leaks, Tikhomirov and Oshanina kept to themselves the truth about Degaev and the plans they had for him: they did not inform the revolutionaries inside Russia what Degaev had confessed lest a spy in their ranks betray the plan to assassinate Sudeikin. Degaev slipped back quietly into St. Petersburg. Apparently his absence had gone unnoticed because one of the radicals residing in the city later insisted that Degaev had been there uninterruptedly throughout May.[43] He was now the unchallenged leader of what was left of the People's Will, and his word was law.

Degaev seemed in no hurry to carry out the instructions given him by Tikhomirov and Oshanina. We can only surmise the reasons for the delay. One may have been his admitted aversion to murder. Because the party members at home had been informed neither of his relationship with Sudeikin nor of his plans to assassinate him, Degaev was on his own, and plotting the murder, as his later actions were to reveal, was beyond his capacity. He also may have wanted to exploit to the fullest his new position in the party, which depended on continued collaboration with Sudeikin. This collaboration took two forms: the launching of a revolutionary press under police supervision and complicity with Sudeikin in preparing a coup d'état. He drew his regular salary of 300 rubles a month, augmented with 1,000 rubles for each trip abroad.[44]

To sow confusion in revolutionary ranks, Sudeikin asked Degaev to start People's Will periodicals which he would censor.[45] In June 1883 M. P. Shebalin printed on a secret press one thousand copies of a new journal, *Listok Narodnoi Voli.* Its ostensible purpose was to demonstrate that despite all blows and the inability to bring out the party's main organ, the *Vestnik,* the organization was alive.[46] Two issues came out, each financed by Sudeikin and approved by him: the first on July 20, 1883, the second on August 20. Sudeikin, in fact, reviewed and occasionally corrected the proofs.[47] He further sponsored, from December 1882 until February 1883, the publication in Geneva of a pseudoanarchist newspaper called *Pravda.*[48] Under Sudeikin's tutelage, the People's Will press also published several pamphlets.

To Shebalin's surprise, Degaev demanded that he insert in the *Listok* an article which praised an anti-Jewish pogrom that had taken place in Ekaterinoslav the previous July, after a Jewish shopkeeper had allegedly beaten up a woman holding a baby who had picked up a weight from his scales. Following this incident, the workers had attacked the Jews, but the government troops came to their defense, allegedly killing as many as two hundred Christians. The article read:

> What will transpire further, we will promptly report, but now we will only remind our readers that the Great French Revolution began with the beating up of Jews (Taine). This is some sort of sad fate which, apparently, cannot be avoided. The Jews, as K. Marx had once beautifully explained, being a nation that is historically unfortunate and for a long time persecuted, have turned into a nation of extreme nervousness and perceptiveness. They repro-

duce in themselves, like a mirror . . . all the vices of
the surrounding milieu, all the curses of a given social order, so that as soon as anti-Jewish movements
begin, one can be assured that they conceal a protest
against the whole order, and signify a much more
profound movement.[49]

Shebalin claimed subsequently that he had objected to Degaev's request as a "provocation," but it duly appeared as a sup-
plement to issue no. 1 of *Listok Narodnoi Voli.*

In fact, the People's Will had more than once in the past
defended anti-Jewish pogroms — whose victims were exclusively poor, small-town Jews — as manifestations of "class con-
sciousness."[50] According to Bogucharskii, "In the newspaper
Narodnaia Volia there not only is definitively not a single item
condemning the pogroms, but . . . responsibility for the pogroms is routinely placed on the Jews themselves."[51] Thus in
August 1881 the Executive Committee had issued an appeal to
the Ukrainian people which said: "The people of the Ukraine
suffer most from the Yids."[52] Apparently, the purpose of this re-
newed appeal to anti-Semitism was to redirect Sudeikin's People's Will organization from terrorism to nationalism.

Sudeikin further sought to replace the genuine People's
Will with a police-sponsored organization under the same
name: it was to convene a congress, change the party's program
to abandon political terrorism, and elect a new Executive Committee. Degaev obliged him by forming a spurious Executive
Committee consisting of himself and four other revolutionaries, which was "known to Sudeikin and operated under his

aegis and with his gracious consent," though none of its members, apart from Degaev, was aware of this fact.[53] It is not clear that it accomplished anything. But had Sudeikin's plot succeeded, it would have replaced the authentic Executive Committee.

In the summer of 1883, unknown to his superiors as well as to the People's Will, Sudeikin became master of the revolution in Russia. In the words of Tikhomirov, "Thus happened something unheard of in the history of the revolutionary movement. The entire revolutionary organization was wholly in the hands of the police, which directed its top management and censored the revolutionary press."[54]

Degaev continued to divulge the identity of revolutionaries, but only erratically: thus we learn from a report of P. Durnovo, the chief of the police, dated December 12, 1884, that in the fall of 1883 he had denounced to the police P. F. Iakubovich, whom he had personally recruited and enrolled in his spurious Executive Committee.[55] But instances are known in which he withheld information from Sudeikin as well as urged suspects to flee abroad to avoid arrest, as ordered by Tikhomirov.[56] He played an intricate and equivocal game to keep at bay alike the police and the terrorists.

To deflect suspicions from Degaev, Sudeikin ordered the murder of a police informer, a laborer by the name of Fedor Shkriaba (also known as Shkrioba). Shkriaba had been apprehended in Kharkov in February 1883 in the roundup of revolutionaries that followed Vera Figner's arrest. In jail he had agreed to collaborate with the police. But as he gave little information, Sudeikin thought him expendable. Sudeikin asked

Degaev to inform the People's Will of Shkriaba's duplicity, and he was duly assassinated on January 8, 1884.[57]

Relying on information provided by Degaev, Sudeikin advised the court that it was safe to proceed with the coronation ceremonies, which had been postponed for an unseemly long time from fear of terrorist outrages.[58] In the nineteenth century, coronations, elaborate rituals performed in the Moscow Kremlin, traditionally took place no later than eighteen months after the death of the reigning monarch, and usually sooner. In the case of Alexander III, nearly two years had elapsed since he had ascended the throne and there still had been no announcement of when the coronation would take place. Now that Sudeikin had given the green light, on January 25, 1883, the court issued a manifesto setting the date for May.[59] Sudeikin went to Moscow to oversee in person the security arrangements. The ceremony took place on May 15 without incident. Sudeikin was rewarded on this occasion with the order of St. Vladimir fourth class, the lowest, which brought with it a supplementary income of 1,200 rubles a year.[60] But he was not promoted in rank, and such treatment only intensified his fury: Degaev's father, a lowly military physician, carried a higher rank than he, the person charged with the security of the empire. Since he had come to St. Petersburg, only one official had lost his life to a terrorist.* And how many terrorist acts had he

---

*On March 18, 1882, General V. S. Strelnikov, the military procurator for the southern region, had been assassinated in Odessa. The revolutionaries hated Strelnikov for his sadism and skill as investigator. Kucharzewski, *Od bialego caratu*, 124–26; V. Burtsev, *Za sto let* (London,

forestalled? Had he not exposed Grachevskii's dynamite factory in St. Petersburg, a potential victim of which was the tsar himself? Yet a whole year has passed since he had received his last promotion.

It is only now, it appears, that Sudeikin ventured on his grand conspiracy: and because his assistance was essential to its success, Degaev agreed to continue to collaborate with him, given that the plot called for the assassination of Tolstoy and other key figures of the regime, which would greatly enhance his reputation among the revolutionaries. Such actions would shake the tsarist government to its foundations and thus realize the aims of the People's Will.

During the six months of their collaboration, Sudeikin and Degaev had become intimate friends. Close in age—Sudeikin was thirty-three at the time, Degaev twenty-six—they addressed each other by the familiar *ty.* They played games. On one occasion, when an "illegal" turned up in St. Petersburg, "Degaev informed Lt. Colonel Sudeikin about him and conveyed the impression that without him Sudeikin would be unable to locate this person, even though he was not without interest to the secret police. Lt. Colonel Sudeikin disagreed and without asking for his address, offered a wager that he would locate him on his own. Degaev accepted the bet, which Lt. Colonel Sudeikin lost because the illegal person, having finished his business, left St. Petersburg."[61] Degaev told Karaulov that Sudeikin occasionally used his apartment for amorous trysts and that on one occasion he found in the water closet

1897), 2: 111; Norman M. Naimark, *Terrorists and Social Democrats* (Cambridge, Mass., 1983), 51–52.

a note "passionate in content," which opened with the words "Dear Georgie."[62] Sudeikin had every reason to trust Degaev, if only because he knew that Degaev would perish at the hands of his comrades were he to divulge their relationship.

Sudeikin now resolved to submit his resignation to the minister of the interior, Tolstoy, following which he planned to engineer, with Degaev's help, assassinations of several important government personalities, beginning with the minister himself, whom he hated with a passion and hoped to replace. The next victims were to have been the tsar's brother, Grand Duke Vladimir, and Konstantin Pobedonostsev, the oberprokuror of the Holy Synod and the tsar's closest confidant. These murders, Sudeikin believed, were certain so to frighten Alexander III that he would promptly recall him to active service on Sudeikin's own terms. He considered the tsar so stupid and weak-willed that he, Sudeikin, would in no time become de facto ruler of the empire. In line with this reasoning, sometime in the early summer of 1883 he was to have asked Tolstoy to relieve him of his duties,[63] but for some reason, perhaps on Tolstoy's urging, decided to postpone his retirement. We possess an undated response of Sudeikin, possibly addressed to his immediate superior, Orzhevskii. Although the circumstances under which it was written are unclear, it is worth quoting because it is one of the very few surviving documents written in his own hand and well reflects the cockiness that made him unpopular in official circles: "I again roar with laughter like a madman. The reason you will be so good as to find in the attached letter. . . . Please note how many directors there are of secret departments, and yet all of you say that I must stay on. . . . But, you, Your Excellency, are pleased to criticize me for

German Lopatin

insufficient discipline."[64] Sudeikin withdrew his petition but insisted that under no condition would he remain on active service beyond May 1884. In the meantime, he provided Degaev with detailed information on Tolstoy's movements.[65] For good measure, he also warned Tolstoy that he was a terrorist target and that he should be especially wary of women petitioners carrying muffs.[66] The thoroughly frightened Tolstoy doubled his protective staff to thirty bodyguards.[67]

Toward the end of the year, Sudeikin connived with Degaev to stage a fictitious attempt on his life, in the course of which he would suffer a minor wound that would justify his immediate retirement or at least lengthy leave of absence. While he was taking a walk in Petrovskii Park, Degaev was to approach him, shoot him in the left hand, and then escape in a carriage that Sudeikin would place nearby.[68] To facilitate the plot, Sudeikin gave him a permit to carry a revolver.

In September 1883 Degaev left on a second trip abroad, this time to Paris. He is said to have done so because Tikhomirov and Oshanina had warned him that unless he carried out his mission of assassinating Sudeikin, they would expose his treachery.[69] Degaev again promised to act, but upon his return home toward the end of the month, he continued to procrastinate.

The fate of Sudeikin was settled with the arrival in St. Petersburg at the end of October or early November of German Lopatin.[70] A veteran revolutionary who had recently escaped from exile, Lopatin had met with Tikhomirov and Oshanina and expressed a desire to become a member of the People's Will. They welcomed his interest but told him nothing about Degaev for fear that such egregious treachery in the party's ranks might discourage him from joining. Against their advice, Lopatin returned to Russia.

Ignorant of Degaev's role, Lopatin met him soon after arriving in the capital. The two had a chat at Palkin's tavern over tea. Lopatin was an expert on escapes—he not only had fled tsarist confinement himself but had successfully sprung Peter Lavrov from Siberian exile. He was struck by inconsistencies in Degaev's account of his past, especially his famous Odessa "escape." Pressed for explanations, Degaev broke down and told him all there was to tell, including the pledge he had given Tikhomirov and Oshanina to kill Sudeikin.[71] "It was an eerie and terrifying moment," Lopatin recalled.[72] Having heard him out, Lopatin insisted that Degaev carry out his promise and from then on exerted on him relentless pressure. He took personal charge of the preparations for the murder although he refused to take part himself.

CHAPTER FIVE

Sudeikin's Murder

The steps leading to the assassination of Sudeikin were set in motion in mid-October 1883, although not much was accomplished until Lopatin's arrival. On October 17–19 Degaev convened a meeting of the spurious People's Will Executive Committee, a gathering of eight Russians and three Poles, to discuss the projected assassination and a number of other issues.[1] The group adopted no formal resolutions, but the drift of its thinking was clear: tactically, it wanted a "review" of terror, and organizationally it called for the dissolution of the Executive Committee in order to strengthen the authority of local revolutionary cells.[2] Sudeikin certainly had every reason to be satisfied with the outcome.

The only participant at this meeting acquainted with Degaev's double role was the twenty-two-year-old Stanislaw Kunicki, a member of the Polish socialist organization Proletariat, who was assigned to escort him during his flight following the murder.* Degaev outlined the plan: he would lure Sudeikin into his apartment and shoot him there. Just how he explained to those unaware of his double role how he would persuade the security chief to pay him a visit cannot be determined. In view of the possibility that at the last moment Degaev's courage might fail him or that he might be overpowered by the much stronger Sudeikin, it was decided that he should have a couple of assistants. Initially, two naval officers were to be assigned this task,[3] but in the end the group settled on the twenty-four-year-old Vasily Petrovich Konashevich (also sometimes spelled Konoshevich), a nobleman and ex-teacher from Poltava, and Nikolai Petrovich Starodvorskii, a twenty-year-old ex-seminarian. Both lived in Kiev under police surveillance and would have been arrested for subversive activities were it not that Sudeikin had instructed the local authorities — possibly on Degaev's advice — not to touch them for the time being.[4] Later in October an emissary of the People's Will from the capital contacted the two men in Kiev and asked them to come to St. Petersburg. They were not told the reason their presence was required: they knew only that there was a "job" to be done. Konashevich did not belong to the People's Will, and Starodvorskii had joined it only recently, but they were quite prepared to kill if the party so desired. On arriving in the capital, they

---

* M. P. Shebalin, in *Narodovol'tsy posle 1-go Marta 1881 goda* (Moscow, 1928), 47. Kunicki belonged to the "self-education" circle which Degaev had formed at the Institute of Transport Engineers in January 1880.

V. P. Konashevich

moved in with the midwife Tatiana Golubeva (Raisa Krantsfeld) on Bol'shaia Sadovaia 114.

The detailed plans of the murder were drawn up and reviewed under Lopatin's supervision in the apartment of the well-known bibliographer S. A. Vengerov.[5] According to Vasily Karaulov, who was close to the events, the projected assassination presented many difficulties, among them Sudeikin's well-known athletic prowess and his habit of carrying one or

N. P. Starodvorskii

more revolvers — which, he boasted, he could fire without missing.[6] As finally worked out, the plan provided that in the event Degaev for any reason failed to dispatch Sudeikin, Konashevich and Starodvorskii would take over and finish him off. Meticulous preparations were made to spirit Degaev out of the country immediately after the murder.

To deflect any suspicions from himself while making these

Vasily Karaulov

preparations, Degaev continued loyally to serve Sudeikin. In October he informed the police about the whereabouts of the terrorist Liudmila Volkenshtein, who four years earlier had taken part in the assassination of the governor of Kharkov, Prince Kropotkin. She was arrested on October 26. This, according to the official police handbook, was the last service that Degaev rendered the secret service.[7] When, a few days later, it was proposed to him that he assist in the search for individuals who had attempted to rob the Kharkov post office, Degaev responded that this was out of the question because his relations with the inspector of the secret police were already known to his previous partners in crime.[8]

In November, Degaev dispatched his wife to Paris, ostensibly to keep an eye on revolutionary émigrés but in fact to place her out of harm's way. She traveled on money and a false passport provided by Sudeikin. Degaev also arranged for his brother to leave for Stockholm; when he departed in early November, Vladimir left behind his common-law wife, Vera Sartori. One week before Sudeikin's murder, Degaev also provided a forged passport for his sister, Liza, but she delayed her departure; when she tried to leave for Stockholm the following February with her husband, Peter Makletsov, both were arrested at the railroad terminal as they were about to board the train.[9] During her interrogation, Liza said that she had once sympathized with the revolutionaries but then "gradually became disenchanted with them because they conspicuously ignored her, isolating her from all participation in the party's work."[10]

Following his wife's departure, on December 3, Degaev moved from the elegant house on Nevskii 105 to a smaller and more modest apartment virtually around the corner, in a house with two exits, one of which gave on Nevskii 91, the other on Goncharnaia 12, across from the Nikolaev railway station.* Located on the third floor and numbered 13, the apartment consisted of four rooms, kitchen and toilet. Here he registered with a false passport furnished by Sudeikin under the name of

---

* The house numbers since then have been changed and today read Nevskii 93 and Goncharnaia 8.

Sergei Petrovich Iablonskii. He had a manservant whom Sudeikin had assigned to him at his request: known as Konstantin, he was a noncommissioned reserve officer whose real name was Pavel Ivanovich Suvorov.

In preparation for the murder, several scenarios were rehearsed. Before her departure for France, Degaev's wife suggested poison, but that was rejected as "degrading."[11] His accomplices considered using daggers but, as they later declared, decided against their use on the grounds that having no experience with daggers, they might inflict unnecessary suffering.[12] More convincing is Lopatin's explanation that daggers would be "unreliable" weapons against a man as strong as Sudeikin[13] and that, furthermore, wounds inflicted with a sharp weapon would provoke shouts that would alert the neighbors. He preferred crowbars on the grounds that "stunning will be silent."[14] On his instructions, Degaev's two accomplices equipped themselves with crowbars, which Starodvorskii purchased at a nearby iron shop: they were twenty-eight inches long and weighed close to eighteen pounds each.

On one occasion, while the preparations were under way, Degaev left the room where Lopatin was coaching Konashevich and Starodvorskii. In his absence, Lopatin told them, jokingly, "Once you have killed Sudeikin, you should also finish off the owner of the apartment." On his return, Degaev asked his two accomplices whether they were clear what to do. "Yes," one of them replied, "once we have disposed of Sudeikin and his companion, we will finish off the owner of the apartment." The frightened Degaev exclaimed, "What, me?" Only then did his accomplices learn that the murder was to take place in Degaev's residence.[15]

Degaev's St. Petersburg apartment, upper right-hand corner

Sometime in the second half of October or in November, Degaev paid an unexpected visit to his sister in Kharkov. He struck her as pale and gloomy: before sitting down to dinner, he asked for vodka, explaining that he could not eat without having something to drink first. It was on this occasion that he told her he intended, with the full approval of the Executive Committee, to kill Sudeikin.[16]

Sudeikin's murder is known to us in great detail from depositions made by Konashevich and Starodvorskii after their arrests in January and March, 1884, respectively.[17] The attempt on Sudeikin's life was scheduled for the afternoon of December 6, three days after Degaev had moved into his new lodgings. He sent his servant Konstantin on an errand to the suburb of Oranienbaum, from which he was not expected to return before evening. Both accomplices were present, armed with crowbars and wearing slippers. It was decided not to resort to gunfire and to rely exclusively on the crowbars to avoid noise: that meant that Degaev would not have to commit the murder which he so dreaded. According to Starodvorskii, it was only then that Degaev informed him and Konashevich of his connections with Sudeikin in order to explain how he had managed to persuade Sudeikin to pay him a visit. But he did not go into details.[18]

Sudeikin had accepted an invitation for 4:00 P.M., but he was late. Ten minutes after the appointed hour, just after Degaev had asked his accomplices to leave, the bell rang. Degaev dashed to the water closet and, standing on the toilet, peeked through the window which gave on the stairwell. Seeing the concierge instead of his expected victim, he did not open the door. After the concierge had left, he heard Sudeikin asking in the courtyard: "Is he home?" and the concierge responding that the tenant was out. At the urging of Konashevich and Starodvorskii, Degaev ran down the stairs, but Sudeikin, who had come in a carriage, was gone.

Degaev, whose nerves were stretched to the limit — one acquaintance who met him shortly before this event was "simply staggered" by the sight of his "pale, contorted face, roving eyes and sickly expression"[19] — now agreed to a proposal by Konashevich. They would revive Sudeikin's own plot to carry out a fake assassination attempt against him while he was taking a stroll in Petrovskii Park, using this opportunity to kill him. But the plot had to be abandoned because Sudeikin, having been warned by his physician that in his case even a slight wound could lead to an erysipelas infection with potentially fatal consequences, changed his mind and dropped the idea.*

The conspirators reverted, therefore, to the original plan. The second attempt took place about a week later, on December 13 or 14. Having fired the revolver indoors and established that the shots could not be heard outside, the conspirators decided to kill Sudeikin that way. But the victim again was late, and Degaev again asked his accomplices to leave. When his guest finally arrived—it was his first visit to Degaev's new quarters—the flustered host concocted a story about a woman from the provinces whom he wanted Sudeikin to meet because she had come to St. Petersburg to carry out a terrorist attack either against the tsar or against him.†

The third and successful attempt occurred on Friday, December 16, around 4:30 P.M., when Degaev had invited Sudeikin to meet the fictitious female terrorist. In the morning of that day, Degaev met on Nevskii with Stepan Rossi, a revolutionary who held Italian citizenship, and asked him to go to Golubeva to remind Starodvorskii to be at his place by 2:00 P.M.[20] From that hour onward the three waited in the bedroom. Degaev, apparently mistrusting himself, told his accomplices that should he once again ask them to leave before Sudeikin had turned up, they were to ignore his request. Konstantin was out. The scheme called on Degaev to shoot Sudeikin as

---

* *NChS* 9 (1925), 211n. Sudeikin had been told that one year earlier, the French statesman Leon Gambetta had died in this manner from an accidental gunshot wound. Ibid., 215.

† Tikhomirov, "V mire," 121. *The Times*, January 25, 1884, p. 6, reported from Russia that Degaev had told Sudeikin he knew of a lady "who was ready to make an attempt on the life of any high functionary."

he entered the study; when, as expected, he would then lurch forward into the bedroom to escape further gunshots, Starodvorskii, concealed there, was to deliver the coup de grâce.

Sudeikin arrived on time, accompanied by Nikolai Dmitrievich ("Koko") Sudovskii, his nephew and a police employee, as athletically built as he. When the bell rang, Konashevich took his assigned place in the kitchen and Starodvorskii in the bedroom. Degaev let the two guests in, locking the door behind them. The apartment was dark, being illuminated by only two candles, one in the living room, the other in the bedroom. Suspecting nothing, Sudeikin took off his coat, in which he carried a revolver; he also put down his walking stick that held a concealed dagger. As he did so, he casually asked: "What about your lady? Has she left?" Degaev, apparently having forgotten the pretext under which he had lured Sudeikin, asked in confusion "What lady?" "Your lady," Sudeikin replied. Degaev led him into the study. Sudovskii stayed behind in the living room, near the entrance to the hall, and lit a cigarette. As Sudeikin entered the study, Degaev fired one shot at his back: aware that Sudeikin always wore a bulletproof vest, he aimed low, at the waist.

Sudeikin, mortally wounded, screamed and shouted to his nephew: "Koko, come here and hit them with the revolver."[21] (Degaev later told Natalie that "in his ears all the time resounded Sudeikin's terrible scream.")[22] But Sudovskii, instead of rushing to his uncle's help, made for the exit. While he was fumbling with the locked door, Konashevich, emerging from the kitchen, struck him with his crowbar. Sudovskii did not fall at once. Konashevich dealt him several more blows on the head, following which Sudovskii dropped to the floor, to all appearances dead.

Sudeikin, instead of plunging into the bedroom, as had been expected, also staggered toward the exit door, with Starodvorskii on his heels. In the living room, he hit Sudeikin on the head, but the blow was a glancing one, and the victim, clutching his left side and screaming, ran into the antechamber. There he turned around to face his pursuer. A blow to the temple finally brought Sudeikin down. Starodvorskii thought him dead, but Sudeikin suddenly jumped to his feet and ran to the water closet. He desperately tried to shut the door, but Starodvorskii held it open with his foot, pulling at the door handle with one hand and with the other battering Sudeikin's hand with the crowbar. When Sudeikin let go and the door swung open, Starodvorskii dealt him another blow on the back of the head. Sudeikin fell forward, and Starodvorskii struck him one more time. Sudeikin collapsed.

Degaev ran away the instant he had fired at Sudeikin: he was in such a hurry, possibly from fear that his accomplices would next turn on him, that he neglected to lock the door. Konashevich walked out shortly after his comrade had killed Sudeikin. Having determined that both police officers were dead, Starodvorskii, candle in hand, carefully inspected the empty apartment to pick up some objects requested by Degaev. He forgot to remove the revolvers, but Degaev had scraped off their serial numbers so that they couldn't be traced to the naval officers who had given them to him. Starodvorskii then locked the door and dropped the key on Nevskii Prospekt. He made his way to the apartment of Raisa Krantsfeld, where he and Konashevich had lived the past month and a half, and there printed an announcement about Sudeikin's murder which Lopatin picked up the next day for distribution. It was brief:

Water closet in Degaev's apartment

Today, Friday, agents of the Execut. Comm. executed the Inspector of the Secret Police, Gendarme
Lieutenant Colonel, G. P. Sudeikin. Killed at the
same time was the detective who protected him.
St. Petersburg, 16 December 1883.[23]

That evening, Lopatin wrote a coded letter to Peter Lavrov in
Paris, asking him to inform Degaev's wife that her husband
had "quit the Crown service in St. Petersburg" and taken a pri-

vate job in the provinces "in the hope of soon getting a foreign assignment." Sudeikin had been killed, he added to Lavrov, but the job had been done "very messily," because both
Degaev and Konashevich had fled the scene of the crime in
haste, leaving the door open. Lopatin implored Lavrov to inform him at once of Degaev's safe arrival: he would not have
peace until he learned that all had ended well.[24] His concern, of
course, stemmed not from fear for Degaev's safety but worry
lest he commit further betrayals. Lopatin left for Paris shortly
afterward.

As previously arranged, Degaev proceeded to an apartment on Zabalkanskii Prospekt which Rossi had asked a friend
to make available to him for the evening and where he awaited
him with a suitcase and forged identity papers. Degaev arrived
in an agitated state around 5:00 P.M. and quickly changed his
clothes; the two then headed for the Warsaw railway terminal.[25] There Rossi turned Degaev over to Kunicki, who was to
accompany him on the voyage south. As they were about to
board, they spotted Konashevich but ignored him: Konashevich boarded the same train but took a seat in another compartment. The two traveled in silence.[26] Kunicki carried a revolver: Lopatin had instructed him, in the event that Degaev
was threatened with arrest or gave any indication of once again
turning traitor, to shoot him in the ear and then commit suicide.[27] That moment seemed about to occur as the train, headed
for Poland, stopped at the Gatchina station longer than scheduled: as Degaev later told his sister, during this nerve-racking
interval he feared he was about to be apprehended.[28]

Fortunately for him, he arrived without hindrance at the
Baltic port city of Libau (Libava, the modern Liepaja). There he

waited while Kunicki left in quest of a false passport. As Degaev later recalled, he boarded the ship that was to take him out of the country with the false passport in one hand and, in the other, concealed in his pocket, a revolver. He passed the gendarme who checked documents. Had the gendarme stopped him, he wrote, it would have been death for both. Kunicki stood on the dock to make sure that all went well.*

Degaev headed for Paris, which he reached a few days after Sudeikin's murder.[29] There he presented himself to a "revolutionary tribunal" consisting of Lopatin, Tikhomirov, and Vasily Karaulov.[30] He offered to commit suicide if such was the party's wish.[31] He further submitted a list of the revolutionaries whom he had betrayed, as well as those whom he considered most dangerous to the party. After his arrest in March 1884, Karaulov told the police that Degaev had revealed the name of every one of Sudeikin's agents in the party organization. He also is said to have turned over handwritten documents by Sudeikin of a "compromising" nature.[32] Shortly afterward, Degaev learned his sentence: his name was dishonored and he was expelled from the party; he was forbidden, under penalty of death, ever to involve himself in its affairs or even to set foot in Russia.[33] He was offered money with which to travel to America.

But Degaev was in no hurry to depart, for he still entertained illusions that he would be readmitted into revolution-

* [W]. Fields [Vladimir Degaev], in *Golos Moskvy*, no. 46 (February 26, 1909). In Feliks Kon's *Vospominaniia* (Moscow, 1935), 38, however, Kunicki is quoted as saying that in Libau he had turned Degaev over to someone else, and with the next train returned to St. Petersburg.

ary ranks. He lingered for at least two years in western Europe, mainly in England.

The shot from Degaev's revolver and the scuffles that followed alerted the residents of the apartment below, and they sent the housemaid to fetch the concierge. Unable to locate him, she dropped into a nearby store to seek help, but the owners said that it was none of their business. Next she went to the local police station. Here she was told: "*This* apartment we do not touch."[34] So nothing was done until late in the evening, around 9:00 P.M., when Degaev's servant, Konstantin, returned home from his errand: unable to enter because he had no key and no one answered the bell, he went in search of help. The police broke into the apartment in the presence of A. F. Dobrzhinskii.

The sight that greeted them was gruesome.[35] The dead Sudeikin lay sprawled on his stomach in the antechamber next to a large pool of blood, head on a raccoon coat, legs inside the water closet. Blood was splattered throughout the apartment. Sudovskii was found dazed, leaning against a chest of drawers in the study: he was promptly taken to a hospital, where he recovered sufficiently the next day to relate what had happened. He is said to have died three days later.[36] The authorities found two revolvers and crowbars, as well as a considerable quantity of illegal literature. The autopsy showed that Sudeikin had suffered four blows on the head, all inflicted from the back. The shot which had pierced his liver was judged fatal.

In government circles, news of Sudeikin's death produced consternation verging on panic: it was the first assassination of

a government official in a year and seemed to portend the re-
surgence of terror. As the London *Times* reported soon after the
event, because nothing "sinister" had occurred for a long time,
government circles believed that "nihilism" had been stamped
out.[37] Peter Valuev, minister of the interior in the previous
reign, noted in his diary on December 19: "Strong impression.
Great alarm." He went on to explain the reason for the anxiety:
Deputy Interior Minister General Orzhevskii, though nomi-
nally in charge of the struggle against the revolution, had entrusted its conduct to Sudeikin: with Sudeikin's death vanished
all the threads that he had held in his hands.[38] Tolstoy was overcome by the news and fully expected to be the next victim:
"I confess," he wrote to Pobedonostsev, "that poor Sudeikin
is constantly on my mind and no matter what I do, he stands
before me. . . . Now these scoundrels intend to kill me. Of
course, my associates are taking every precautionary measure;
but inasmuch as one cannot guarantee success when dealing
with such bandits, therefore, I think, should misfortune befall
me, one should give thought now to the person who could replace me."[39] His nerves were shattered, and in 1884–85 he left
St. Petersburg for half a year.[40]

Drawing on evidence supplied by Sudovskii from his hospital bed, Tolstoy notified the tsar of the crime. Alexander III
responded: "I am terribly *shocked* and *distressed* by this news.
Of course, we have always feared for Sudeikin, but now a
treacherous death. — A loss that is positively irreplaceable! Who
now will take on such a duty [?] Please, send me all news that
will be discovered about this murder."[41] Indeed, no one could
replace Sudeikin, and the post of inspector, which he had held
during the past year, was abolished.

Sudeikin was buried with great honors. The funeral, which took place on December 20, was attended by some dignitaries, including ministers, but mostly by members of the security services. The empress sent a wreath made of white lilies — symbols of innocence — with the inscription: "To him who has fulfilled his sacred duty." The body was taken to the Nikolaev railway station, across from the building where he had been murdered, and conveyed through Moscow to the Orlov province, where it was interred.[42] Sudeikin's widow received a lifelong annual state pension of five thousand rubles and the promise that her three children would be educated at the state's expense.[43]

Toward the end of February 1884 the authorities took the unprecedented step of distributing nationwide thousands of posters carrying Degaev's likeness and offering rewards of up to ten thousand rubles for information leading to his arrest. It was the first time that the tsarist government had turned to the public for help in apprehending a criminal.[44] The posters showed six facial likenesses: three of Degaev with hat and three without hat, two with beard, two with mustache, and two cleanly shaven.[45]

In early March 1884 the police already knew of Degaev's flight to Paris and of his "trial." This they learned from the deposition of Karaulov, who had returned to Kiev to open a printing press but was promptly arrested and spoke quite freely.

Degaev's family was immediately placed under surveillance, which continued for several years. One sister was imprisoned, another exiled from St. Petersburg, while Natalia Mekletsova and her husband were subjected to repeated searches.[46] All were ostracized by society. Degaev learned to his deep distress

ОБЪЯВЛЕНІЕ.

ОТСТАВНОЙ ШТАБСЪ-КАПИТАНЪ

СЕРГѢЙ ПЕТРОВЪ ДЕГАЕВЪ

Примѣты: Маленькаго роста, худощавый, темный блондинъ.

обвиняется въ убійствѣ 16-го Декабря 1883 года Подполковника Судейкина.

5,000 РУБЛЕЙ

назначено за сообщеніе полиціи свѣдѣній, которыя, давъ возможность опредѣлить мѣстонахожденіе Дегаева, поведутъ къ его задержанію.

10,000 РУБЛЕЙ

будутъ выданы тому, кто, указавъ полиціи мѣстопребываніе Дегаева, окажетъ содѣйствіе къ задержанію преступника.

Poster with reward for help in Degaev's apprehension

that one of his sisters had been publicly insulted in the theater by an acquaintance.[47]

The revolutionaries, of course, were overjoyed. Lopatin informed Lavrov five days after the event that "the liberal public is very happy with what had happened, seeing in it the beginning of new vigorous activity, and asks: 'and when Tolstoy?'"[48] Stepniak wrote in the London *Daily News* eleven days after the event that it provided "brilliant proof" of the strength of the People's Will.[49] In reality, of course, it did nothing of the kind: the elusive gendarme was assassinated not by the People's Will but by an agent of the police who had turned against his superior in an act of triple betrayal. On February 26, 1884, the People's Will issued a warning that it would kill anyone cooperating with the authorities' request to help capture Sudeikin's assassins.[50]

Degaev's betrayals had a more profound and lasting effect on the revolutionary cause than the loss of many members. As no. 10 of *Narodnaia Volia,* finally issued in September 1884, reported: "The accursed 'Degaevshchina' in a fateful way left its terrible moral traces in the decline of party discipline and the weakening of mutual trust among the party's members."[51] In fact, the party never recovered from these blows.

The police authorities undertook intense searches. In January 1884 they dispatched to Switzerland Peter Rachkovskii, who in time would become a leading official of the Okhrana's foreign branch and ultimately its director. His first assignment was to locate Degaev's wife.[52]

After a brief stay in Paris, Degaev moved to London, where he lived in deep concealment. He was evidently very confused about his status in the revolutionary movement. He conceded that had been guilty of unforgivable wrongs and yet expected from his comrades not only understanding and forgiveness but even approval. Strange as it may seem, he thought that his killing Sudeikin should atone for all his previous sins and that he had the right to be treated as a hero. Oshanina wrote that he "suffered from a mania of grandeur and even when discussing his vile deeds he seems to have expected admiration or, at any rate, astonishment at the steadfastness of his character, his self-possession, his ability to wear a mask, etc."[53] N. M. Salova, who knew him well, agreed: "[Degaev], in my opinion, was not an ordinary traitor concerned only with self-advantage. He was also a psychopath, suffering from *folie de grandeur*."[54] His brother Vladimir, defending him from charges of cowardice, wrote in 1909: "No one would have been capable of spending two years in the conditions under which he lived in St. Petersburg in 1882–83 unless endowed with an iron will and fearlessness."[55]

He was grievously disappointed in his expectations.

"My situation is really terribly difficult," he wrote to Oshanina on January 29, 1884: "I see that everyone has turned decisively against me and [people] apparently even look at me with revulsion. Of course, I am very guilty."[56] Later that year Vladimir wrote Tikhomirov that his brother lived in a state of despair: "He suffers terribly, cannot sleep at night and when he does fall asleep sees the faces of those who are imprisoned because of him and must quickly wake up to regain his calm. He suffers acutely for his family from whom, because of him, everyone has turned away — radicals but also, as he learns from his sister's letters, completely uninvolved, ordinary people."[57]

He was disturbed by the articles which Russian revolutionary émigrés published in the English press. He was especially upset by a mention of him in an article by Tikhomirov (whom he admired) in the December 1884 issue of the English Marxist monthly *To-Day,* which referred to him as a "villain" who had taken advantage of Vera Figner's "trusting nature."[58] In January 1885 he wrote Tikhomirov in the partly confused, partly coded language that characterized all his writings:

> From the letters of my brother, and also from newspaper articles and the article in *To-day,* I see, to my astonishment, that in the eagerness to defend yourself from accusations of naïveté, you turn me into some kind of *Van'ka*-Cain in the eyes of the English public.* I will say nothing against the article in *Narodnaia Volia* which appeared in Russia[59] — perhaps there it was necessary to depict the entire affair as inspired only by self-interested calculations, but you, you *know* that it was much more complicated. It seems to me that it was enough to say that "I was once a revolutionary," that you do not know precisely all the facts to judge. But to say that this villain first betrayed that woman [Vera Figner] who, in her innocence, had trusted him (probably others, too, had trusted him), and the deceased [Sudeikin] had trusted, this means to betray me into the hands of the Russian government. Because this means that

---

* *Van'ka*-Cain: a play on the expression *van'ka-vstan'ka,* a person who always talks himself out of trouble.

there was no political element present. There was villainy; a man who has betrayed his friends thinks nothing of killing another human being. Gentlemen, believe me, all these "loathings" mean nothing to me. I do not like martyrdom, I *have to* harm that which I consider the worst scum—i.e., the people who govern Russia. If my fact did not turn out fully grandiose, did not inspire horror, then the responsibility lies not only on me but in my being alone.*
If at that time I had had comrades in this matter and preparation, then it would have turned out differently. You *know* and *believe* that I was not a revolutionary for the last time, and for this reason do not spoil my plans, otherwise I will defend myself, if only, for instance, [by revealing] that others too are just as guilty of "knowing and not denouncing" as I am. Forget about me until I again remind of myself. But if *you* must publicly express indignation, then do it in such a way that the deed includes some politics, and not only villainy.[60]

Tikhomirov interpreted the threat contained in this letter to mean that Degaev accused his one-time comrades of portraying the murder of Sudeikin as an ordinary, nonpolitical crime, because such a crime would leave him liable to be extradited to Russia. His threat, as Tikhomirov interpreted it, was that in that event he would defend himself by naming others—presumably Tikhomirov, first and foremost, but also Lopatin,

* "My fact": the murder of Sudeikin.

and Oshanina as others who also had known about and failed to denounce the crime.[61]

Some time in 1886 Degaev apparently concluded that he could expect nothing from his one-time comrades but more abuse and ostracism, and in order to start a new life, he sailed with his wife for North America.* His whereabouts during the next decade are hard to ascertain because he lived in constant fear of denunciation and went to great lengths to conceal his whereabouts. As a rule, he communicated with the outside world through his brother, who also emigrated to the United States.

It is said that the Degaevs first made their home in Canada, where Sergei, fluent in French, got various low-paying jobs while his wife worked as cook and laundress.[62] Having in the meantime learned English, he moved to the United States, where he found employment as a superintendent with a chemical firm in St. Louis, a position he held for nine years. In 1891, while thus employed, he enrolled in an informal course of mathematics given by Professor C. M. Woodward at Washington University in St. Louis. On September 4 of that year he and his wife were naturalized in St. Louis under the family name Pell—he as Alexander, she as Emma.† Four years later,

---

*M. P. Shebalin, *Klochki vospominanii* (Moscow, 1935), 161, heard from Karaulov that the Degaevs had left for South America; this is confirmed by N. M. Salova in *Granat*, vol. 40, 403. But there exists no other independent evidence for this allegation.

†Hardesty and Unruh, 14. Degaev may have adopted the name from John Pell, a famous English mathematician of the seventeenth century. Another possibility is his contemporary, Aleksandr Vasilevich Pel', a prominent Russian chemist.

with Professor Woodward's support, he applied for a course of graduate study at Johns Hopkins. He completed his studies in two years and in June 1897 received the doctorate. In the fall of that year, he left for South Dakota.

Epilogue

All that remains now to complete the story of Degaev is to trace his final years, as well as the fate of those Russians who had been involved in his extraordinary life. For the most part, it is a melancholy tale.

Degaev's beloved wife, Liubov, rechristened Emma, died in December 1904. Three years later, at the age of fifty, Pell married one of his students, Anna Johnson, a gifted young mathematician half his age. The marriage took place in Göttingen, where his future wife was studying. It was presumably to be near her—she enrolled as a graduate student at the University of Chicago—that in August 1908 he resigned from the University of South Dakota and accepted an appointment as assistant professor of mathematics at the Armour Institute in Chicago (later renamed the Illinois Institute of Technology). In 1910 his new wife became "the first woman and only the second [female] University of South Dakota graduate" to earn a doctorate.[1]

Appearances to the contrary, Degaev lived in constant fear of revolutionary retribution, especially after April 1906, when a new Russian periodical *Byloe (The Past),* dedicated to the history of the Russian revolutionary movement, published articles about him and reproduced the government poster offering a reward for his capture. His anxiety increased when he learned that during that year a radical youth killed one F. E. Kuritsyn, who in the distant 1870s had served as a police informer.[2] In 1909, to throw potential avengers off his brother's track, Vladimir told a Russian newspaper that Sergei had died in New Zealand in August 1908 after a "fairly brilliant" mathematical career in the United States, New Zealand, and Australia.[3]

In 1911 Degaev suffered a heart attack. Two years later he resigned from the Armour Institute and gave up teaching. He accompanied his wife to Mount Holyoke, where she taught from 1913 to 1918, and from there moved with her to Bryn Mawr, where she chaired the mathematics department. By this time she was one of America's leading women mathematicians.

During World War I, Russian émigrés tracked Degaev to the vicinity of New York. According to the account of Lev Deich, after some hesitation they decided not to betray him for sins committed long in the past. Deich felt pangs of conscience for an article he had once written in which he had revealed that Kuritsyn had once worked for the police, as a result of which Kuritsyn, who had become a peaceful citizen, was assassinated.[4]

In 1918, half a year after the Bolsheviks had taken power, another announcement of Degaev's death appeared in the Russian press. This time he was said to have been killed in the United States by a group of "Internationalists-Terrorists."[5]

In reality, he died peacefully in bed on January 26, 1921. His last recorded words, written in 1918, soon after the Bolshevik regime had proclaimed the "Red Terror," were: "Accursed Russia, even after liberating herself, she does not let people live . . ."[6]

His widow, who remarried, established a fund in Pell's name at the University of South Dakota which to this day pays out a modest scholarship.

•

Vladimir Degaev, after spending some time in Stockholm, moved to Paris, where he is said to have played the stock market with some success. In 1888 he emigrated to the United States. After working for the Equitable Insurance Company, he took a job as secretary of the Russian consul general in New York City. His task was to keep an eye on Russian émigrés, especially anarchists.[7] He married an American woman with whom he had four children.[8] He maintained contact with Sergei and defended him from charges of cowardice and treachery. He contributed to Russia's leading reactionary newspaper, *Novoe Vremia*, under the pen name "W. Fields" (an adaptation of his mother's maiden name, Polevoi, the root of which — *pole* — means "field"). His articles were full of anti-Semitic remarks: to a journalist who questioned him about them, he confessed that, indeed, he did hate "Yids."[9] The "good, gentle" lad with a "childishly pure" soul had apparently changed a great deal since leaving Russia.

Natalie also stayed in touch with her brother and in the summer of 1906 published an article in *Byloe* in which, without defending his past actions, she attempted to portray him in a more favorable light.[10] She seems to have met with him on at least one occasion in western Europe.

Liza fared poorly. Unable to hold on to a job, she blamed the authorities, accusing them of punishing her for the sins of her brother. In fact, she was jobless because of chronic tardiness. The police reported in June 1893 that she had offered on several occasions to reveal the whereabouts of her brother if properly rewarded. But by then interest in him had waned and the reward offered in 1884 had been withdrawn.[11]

Lev Tikhomirov, the principal theoretician of the People's

Will, broke with the revolutionaries in the late 1880s. He first underwent a religious conversion and then a political one, having decided that autocracy was the proper form of government for Russia. He recanted his previous views and in August 1888, in a letter to Plehve, the head of the police department, asked to be forgiven and allowed back to Russia.[12] He wrote several books to explain his motivation. Terror, he argued in *Why I Ceased to Be a Revolutionary,* was futile: either the revolutionaries had enough public support to launch a revolution, in which case it was unnecessary, or they did not, in which case it was useless.[13] In 1909 he became editor-publisher of a leading daily, *Moskovskie Vedomosti,* which under his editorship became so reactionary that he was dismissed from the post. By 1913 he was a full-fledged member of the tsarist establishment, holding the rank of state counselor and working for the main censorship bureau. He stayed in Russia after the revolution and died there in dire poverty in 1923.

Of the people who had helped Degaev set up the Odessa printing press, Spandoni spent the years 1883 to 1902 in hard labor and exile. In 1905 he drew another sentence of three years' exile. He died the following year. The sixteen-year-old Kaliuzhnaia was released from prison after short detention, which gave rise to rumors that she had turned informer. It appears that these rumors were deliberately spread by the gendarmes. To clear her name, she shot the Odessa gendarme officer A. Katanskii. Sentenced to hard labor in the Kara penal colony, she committed suicide after one of the female prisoners there had been subjected to corporal punishment that resulted in her death.[14]

The two accomplices of Degaev were arrested soon after

Sudeikin's murder: Konashevich on January 3, 1884, in Kiev, Starodvorskii on March 16, 1884, in Moscow.[15] They were sentenced in 1887 to twenty-six and twenty-two years, respectively, in the Schlüsselburg fortress.[16] Konashevich went insane and in 1896 was transferred to a prison psychiatric hospital in Kazan,[17] where he died in 1915. Starodvorskii in 1889 wrote to the director of police from prison that he was a monarchist at heart. Amnestied in 1905, he turned into a paid police informer. Later he changed colors again and in 1917 served as a revolutionary commissar: at his death in 1925 he was eulogized by the Bolsheviks for having spent so many years in tsarist prisons.[18] Rossi, who had helped Degaev escape, was arrested while attending Sudeikin's funeral. He promptly went on the police payroll: it was his information that led to the arrest of Konashevich and Starodvorskii.[19] Kunicki, who had escorted Degaev out of St. Petersburg after the murder, was arrested in Warsaw in June 1884 and hanged in January 1886.[20]

Vasily Karaulov, who had been close to Degaev and Lopatin, returned to Russia in February 1884, and on March 4 was apprehended in Kiev as he was about to set up a printing press. He spoke freely to the gendarme officials, revealing that Degaev was in Paris. He also disclosed that Sudeikin and Degaev had plotted a fake assault on Sudeikin. Wanting to provide for his family, he seemed tempted to disclose Degaev's specific whereabouts by the promise of a 10,000-ruble reward, but then he backed off.[21] Sentenced to four years of hard labor, after his release he turned against the revolutionaries. Amnestied in 1906, he was elected deputy of the liberal Constitutional-Democratic Party to the Third Duma. He died in 1910.[22]

Lopatin, who had supervised the murder of Sudeikin, was

arrested in St. Petersburg in October 1884. A search of his person turned up a notebook containing the names and addresses of active members and sympathizers of the People's Will, which enabled the police to seize some five hundred persons.[23] This marked the end of the People's Will. Lopatin spent eighteen years in the Schlüsselburg fortress before being released in the general amnesty proclaimed after October 17, 1905. He died in 1918.

Of Sudeikin's children, the only one on whom there is information is his youngest, Sergei Iurevich, who became an artist and achieved modest success as a designer of sets and costumes for the Soviet stage.

The last word shall be given to Vera Figner. She was sentenced to death in 1884, but her sentence was commuted to hard labor. She spent the next twenty years at Schlüsselburg, displaying throughout remarkable courage and integrity. She outlived virtually every other member of the People's Will, witnessing the October revolution, collectivization, the Great Terror, and the first year of the Soviet-German war. In 1921–22 she published her memoirs, but in general she kept quiet and stayed out of trouble. She died in Moscow in 1942 at the age of ninety.

Sometime during the difficult winter of 1917–18, when the Bolsheviks were imposing their dictatorship on a country that had barely tasted freedom, a group of Russian intellectuals met at the home of A. M. Kalmykova, a socialist who in the 1890s had been active in educational work. The guests had connections in various European countries. The hostess asked the assembled company to appeal to Europe in the name of the Russian intelligentsia that the Bolsheviki were not representatives of the working class, but impostors and demagogues, who exploited base instincts. Two or three of those present said something. Then V. Figner spoke up. Lowering her eyelids, she began by saying that there was no point in turning to Europe with a complaint against ourselves. That which was occurring in Russia was the work of our own hands, because we have taught, we have preached precisely that which the Bolsheviks and the masses that follow them are now doing.[24]

From the Executive Committee of the People's Will

The document which follows, dated December 21, 1883 — five days after Sudeikin's murder — but published only in September 1884, was almost certainly written by Lev Tikhomirov, immediately after the "trial" of Degaev by the three-member Executive Committee of the People's Will.* Although its author attempts to portray the People's Will as much stronger and effective than it in fact was, the document deserves attention for two reasons: the proclamation gives an account of the motives that Degaev gave to the Executive Committee, and it further reveals the reasoning behind the committee's treatment of Degaev after he had confessed to his betrayals.

•

---

* *Narodnaia Volia,* no. 10 (September 1884), 1–3, reprinted in *Literatura Partii "Narodnoi Voli"* (Moscow, 1930), 211–13.

In view of the many—mostly false—rumors about the facts connected with the execution of Sudeikin, the Executive Committee of the party of the People's Will deems it a duty toward its comrades and the public at large to publish on this subject the following:

From our previous publications, it is known that the Executive Committee decided not to carry out any offensive operations prior to the appearance of the Coronation Manifesto of Alexander III, leaving it up to the Russian government itself to demonstrate to the Russian people that even when not perturbed by the blows of the revolutionaries it was incapable of taking any beneficial measures for Russia. The execution of Strelnikov, prepared beforehand, was only a particular measure of self-defense.*

But this deliberate inactivity, which, owing to the unprecedented cowardice of Alexander III, exceeded all the reckonings and assumptions of the Executive Committee and extended over too long a time, was interpreted not only by enemies of the People's Will but also by some of its members as a consequence of the party's debility caused by the major blows previously inflicted on it. This could have occurred especially in the case of some individuals who occupied secondary posts in the organization—posts which did not permit them to acquire proper knowledge of its intentions and strengths—and, who finding themselves afterward in prison or exile, cut off from live contacts with the comrades, could have had only the most inadequate knowledge of what the Committee did or

* See page 88, footnote.

planned to do at the time. Such a faint-hearted, distrustful attitude toward the inner strength of our cause and the forces available to the party defending it, linked to an unfortunate personality made up of a misshapen blend of immense self-confidence and conceit along with a contemptible fear for one's own safety and well-being, led, in one case, to a succession of deplorable and simply criminal actions which inflicted on our party a great deal of irreparable harm and, for a time, really paralyzed its activity.

We are referring, of course, to S. P. Degaev, a man who joined the party at the time of its might, who carried out many tasks entrusted to him and who, consequently, at the time of subsequent routs, rose fairly high in the organizational hierarchy, despite the fact that his past, deficient in serious tests, did not give the needed guarantees that at other times, under all conditions, he would display absolute fortitude.

Arrested in Odessa in December 1882, feeling himself most seriously compromised, frightened by the prospect of personal destruction that opened up before him, under the influence of prison illusions and his own weak character faint-heartedly confusing his own destruction and impotence with the destruction and impotence of the cause and the party, and superstitiously imagining Sudeikin's police that had seized him to be an omnipotent and omnipresent force, he decided on a plan of action that not only would deliver him from hard labor but also open up before him, as he saw it, the alluring perspective of a brilliant political role. Finding himself in a condition of spiritual gloom and moral collapse, cut off from the moral support of stronger and nobler personalities, he conceived the notion of purchasing the gratitude and confidence of the government at the price of betraying his erstwhile friends and its worst enemies in order subsequently, after he had gained the full confidence of autocratic power, to deliver to it, when the occasion arose, a decisive blow. With these chimerical, confused, and profoundly immoral ideas in his head, he proffered Sudeikin his services. These were eagerly accepted by the frightened government, which instantly arranged for him a spurious escape, that delivered once again this unconscionable and dangerous enemy into [the party's] ranks.

If one is to believe his own explanations, he flattered himself for a time with the hope that he would attain his objective at the price of relatively insignificant sacrifices, betraying only undertakings and individuals of secondary importance, while safeguarding the most important activists and all important undertakings and institutions, and even assuring the latter of greater progress under his personal protection. But reality soon crushed these fantastic plans and demonstrated fully how chimerical was the unprincipled and criminal escapade. Under the constant pressure of the insatiable police and under the constant danger of losing its confidence and awakening suspicions of himself, he was compelled, step by step, to betray to it almost all that he knew, sparing neither his personal friends or acquaintances who trusted him, nor institutions and undertakings of the greatest importance, except those that were unknown to him by virtue of his position in the hierarchy. Moreover, under the pressure of the same motives and to confer on himself greater importance and a more secure position, he even invented nonexistent undertakings and attributed to many individuals, even those who did not belong at all to the organization, a completely fantastic prominence.

But all this, of course, led nowhere, and having destroyed many serious undertakings and caused the ruin of not a few noble individuals, he was unable to extricate himself from the most disgraceful role of an ordinary traitor and spy.

And now, crushed by the awareness of his criminal self-deception, unwittingly yielding to the influence of his restored moral atmosphere, tormented by the pangs of conscience, despairing not only of a brilliant but of any career, kept by the government in the unenviable position of a police bloodhound, constantly afraid lest his shameful secret be revealed, and, finally, exhausted by the constant struggle against suspicions of him, he decided, in the end, to make a confession to the Executive Committee, leaving it up to the Committee either to sentence him to a well-deserved execution or to allow him to expiate, if only to a certain extent, his crime with some service to the party.

Confronting this profoundly sad and tragic task, the Executive Committee, as the representative of a political party, felt it had no right to act as would a private person in everyday life and let itself be guided in its decision solely by moral probity and the demands of abstract justice. On the contrary: it assumed that its direct duty was to ensure—by physical death or other means—the full annihilation of the person of Degaev for the party, the government, and society, while at the same time achieving certain important objectives. Namely, it found it necessary: 1. first and foremost, to save those active agents who, although betrayed to the police, remained still at liberty;

2. to withdraw from police surveillance those institutions which had been revealed to it and to conceal them in a fully reliable manner; 3. to obtain from Degaev detailed information about all the hired agents and voluntary accomplices of the political police; and 4. to execute Sudeikin himself (but, without fail, by Degaev personally), because, in the opinion of the Committee, this indefatigable sower of political debauchery should perish in the same pit which he had dug for others, teaching, with his death, an eternally memorable lesson that everything based on treason has no future. And only such mutual annihilation of the two individuals deserving one another, could, in the Committee's opinion, assuage at least to some extent the indignant moral feeling of the spectators of this tragedy, and truly ensure that in the future Degaev would not reappear on this or that side of Russian political life. There is no need to add that all betrayals have absolutely ceased from the instant Degaev had placed himself at the disposal of the Executive Committee.

As concerns the enforcement of the Committee's orders affecting the execution of Sudeikin, this is sufficiently known to each and all from various newspapers. Compelled by bitter necessity to overcome its moral squeamishness and legitimate indignation and resort to Degaev's services, the Executive Committee found it fair to commute [Degaev's] capital punishment to definitive expulsion from the party, forbidding him, under the threat of death, ever to appear in the ranks of the Russian revolutionary movement. The Executive Committee invites all members of the People's Will organization to keep an eye on the exact enforcement of this sentence, as well as on the behavior of other persons stained by deals with Sudeikin, Plehve, and the police at large.

Let these people know that the organization has been warned about their escapades, and that at present the only way out for them is voluntarily to return to private life. Notwithstanding all the importance of the objectives which preoccupy it, the Executive Committee will find the time steadfastedly to pursue the task of purifying the Russian political atmosphere of the demoralization, which Sudeikin had fostered in it.

The Executive Committee

21 December 1883

Notes

ONE
Alexander Pell

1. Cedric Cummins, *The University of South Dakota, 1862–1966* (Vermillion, S.D., 1975), 1–10.
2. *The Coyote '03* (Vermillion, S.D.), June 1902, 13.
3. Lewis E. Akeley, *This Is What We Had in Mind* (Vermillion, S.D., 1959), 59.
4. Lewis E. Akeley, in *Alumni Quarterly of the University of South Dakota* 17, no. 1 (April 1921), 29.
5. Ibid., 31.
6. Quoted in Hardesty and Unruh, 23–24. This is the fullest account of Pell's years at the University of South Dakota.
7. Akeley, *This Is What We Had in Mind,* 61–62.
8. Salary: Hardesty and Unruh, 23.
9. Ibid., 20–21.
10. Akeley, in *Alumni Quarterly,* 31.
11. Hardesty and Unruh, 16.
12. *Coyote '03,* 20.
13. *Biographia Literaria,* chapter 11.

TWO
Sergei Degaev

1. A. P. Pribyleva-Korba, *Narodnaia Volia* (Moscow, 1926), 161.
2. Ibid., 161–62; Tikhomirov, "Neizdannye," 167.
3. Tikhomirov, "Neizdannye," 167.
4. Figner, *Trud,* 340.
5. GARF, Fond 102, 3 DP, 1879, delo 58, list 3.
6. Appendix to *Obzor,* January 1, 1881–July 1, 1881, 9–10, Nikolaevsky Archive, Hoover Institution. March 15 was two weeks after the assassination of Alexander II.
7. Ibid., 23, 28.

8. *Byloe,* no. 8 (August 1906), 160.

9. Ibid., 161.

10. Figner, *Trud,* 341.

11. S. A. Ivanov, in *Narodovol'tsy 80-kh i 90-kh godov* (Moscow, 1929), 54.

12. Figner, *Trud,* 338.

13. M. P. Shebalin, *Letuchaia tipografiia "Narodnoi Voli" v 1883 g.* (Moscow, 1926), 22.

14. Ibid., 21.

15. Tikhomirov, "Neizdannye," 167.

16. Figner, *Trud,* 341.

17. Shebalin, *Letuchaia tipografiia,* 23.

18. On the terrorists' mental instability, see A. I. Solzhenitsyn, *Dvesti let vmeste (1795–1995)* (Moscow, 2001), 224, referring to Lev Deich, *Rol' evreev v russkom revoliutsionnom dvizhenii,* vol. 1, 2d ed. (Moscow, 1925).

19. *Vospominaniia L'va Tikhomirova* (Moscow and Leningrad, 1927), 129.

20. Ibid., 131.

21. Quoted in M. N. Polonska-Oshanina in *Byloe,* no. 6/18 (1907), 7.

22. Figner, *Trud,* 285.

23. Lev Tikhomirov, *Pochemu ia perestal byt' revoliutsionerom* (Moscow, 1895), 46–47.

24. Vladimir Burtsev, *Bor'ba za svobodnuiu Rossiiu: Moi vospominaniia (1882–1922)* (Berlin, 1923), 1: 41.

25. O. V. Aptekman, *Obshchestvo "Zemlia in Volia 70-kh gg."* (Petrograd, 1924), 144–45.

26. Vladimir Burtsev, *Za sto let* (London, 1897), 1: 151.

27. Kucharzewski, *Od bialego caratu,* 115.

28. Quoted in Richard Pipes, *Russia Under the Old Regime* (London, 1974), 293. Emphasis added.

29. Burtsev, *Za sto let,* 1: 180.

30. *Financial Times,* July 21–22, 2001, p. iii.

31. Pribyleva-Korba, *Narodnaia Volia,* 168.

32. GARF, Fond 102, 3 DP, opis' 1881, delo 550, list 16.

THREE
Lieutenant Colonel Sudeikin

1. The biographical data which follow come from Sudeikin's service record compiled on January 4, 1884, and deposited in GARF, Fond 110, opis' 17, delo 92, lista 256–61.
2. Jonathan W. Daly, *Autocracy Under Siege* (De Kalb, Ill., 1998), 55.
3. A. P. Martynov, *Moia sluzhba v otdel'nom korpuse zhandarmov* (Stanford, Calif., 1972), 7.
4. L. G. Deich, *Provokatory i terror: Po lichnym vospominaniiam* (Tula, 1926), 17.
5. Emile Gaboriau, *Monsieur Lecoq* (New York, 1975), 14–15.
6. *Dnevnik gosudarstvennogo sekretaria A. A. Polovtsova; 1883–1892* (Moscow, 1966), 1: 157.
7. Tikhomirov, "V mire," 92.
8. *Obschee Delo*, no. 58 (January–February, 1884), 12.
9. M. R. Popov, *Zapiski zemlevol'tsa* (Moscow, 1933), 264.
10. Stepniak in *Obschee Delo*, no. 58 (January–February, 1884), 12.
11. P. S. Ivanovskaia, *V Boevoi Organizatsii: Vospominaniia* (Moscow, 1929), 141.
12. Stepniak-Kravchinskii, in *Obschee Delo*, 12.
13. Ibid., 13.
14. O-ia [Pelagiia Ia. Osmolovskaia], in *Nasha Strana: Istoricheskii Sbornik*, no. 1 (1907), 307.
15. N. A. Troitskii in *VI*, no. 3 (1976), 125–26; G. Golovkov and S. Burin, *Kantselariia nepronitsaemoi t'my* (Moscow, 1994), 47.
16. Golovkov and Burin, *Kantselariia*, 45.
17. Lev Tikhomirov, *Zagovorshchiki i politsiia* (Moscow and Leningrad, 1928), 203.
18. *Vol'noe Slovo* (Geneva), no. 41 (July 15, 1882), 3.
19. Daly, *Autocracy Under Siege*, 83.
20. Tikhomirov, "V mire," 106.
21. [Alexander Dębski], "Wspomnienia o Kunickim i Bardowskim," *Z pola walki* (London, 1904), 84.
22. Peregudova, *Sysk*, 18.
23. Norman M. Naimark, *Terrorists and Social Democrats* (Cambridge, Mass., 1983), 17.

24. S. S. Volk, *Narodnaia Volia* (Moscow and Leningrad, 1966), 142–43.

25. Vl. Debogorii-Mokrievich in *Byloe*, no. 4/16 (April, 1907), 56–61.

26. Vl. Burtsev, *Za sto let* (London, 1897), 1: 178.

27. On Dobrzhinskii, see *KA*, no. 5/30 (1928), 181.

28. Ibid., 165.

29. Ludwik Bazylow, *Działalność Narodnictwa Rosyjskiego w Latach 1878–1881* (Wrocław, 1960), 135.

30. Tikhomirov, *Zagovorshchiki*, 100–102.

31. *KA*, no. 5/30 (1928), 137.

32. *To-Day*, no. 6 (June 1884), 403–4.

33. Figner, *Trud*, 366.

34. Iurii Davydov, *Glukhaia pora listopada* (Moscow, 1999), 570. Although Davydov's book is historical fiction, one reviewer confirmed that this quotation came from an actual letter sent by a prisoner: F. Svetov in *Novyi Mir*, no. 12 (1968), 233.

35. *Delo provokatora Okladskogo* (Leningrad, 1925), 12.

36. Ibid., 135–36.

37. Ivanovskaia, *V Boevoi Organizatsii*, 140–42. Henry Maudsley was a nineteenth-century English psychologist, Cesare Lombroso an Italian physician and psychiatrist.

38. Quoted in O-ia [Pelagiia Ia. Osmolovskaia], in *Nasha Strana*, 301.

39. K. Ia. Zagorskii in *KiS*, no. 3/76 (1931), 156–79.

40. Ibid., 174–75.

41. Figner, *Trud*, 340.

42. A. P. Pribyleva-Korba, *Narodnaia Volia* (Moscow, 1926), 164.

43. Ibid.; Deich, *Provokatory i terror*, 9.

44. On Kletochnikov, see N. Troitskii in *Prometei*, no. 9 (1972) 57–76.

45. Kletochnikov's reports for the year 1879 are reprinted in *Arkhiv "Zemli i Voli" i "Narodnoi Voli"* (Moscow, 1932), 160–234.

46. *Vospominaniia L'va Tikhomirova* (Moscow, 1927), 130.

47. Golovkov and Burin, *Kantselariia*, 25.

48. Pribyleva-Korba, *Narodnaia Volia*, 164–65.

49. Date from *Narodovol'tsy posle 1-go Marta 1881 goda* (Moscow, 1928), 164.

50. Deich, *Provokatory i terror*, 8.

51. Pribyleva-Korba, *Narodnaia Volia*, 171.

52. GARF, Fond 102, 3 DP, opis' 78, 1882, delo 506. Degaeva's deposition: GARF, Fond 102, 7 DP, 1884, delo 747, ch. 12, t. 2, list 13.

53. F[eliks] Lure, *Politseiskie i provokatory* (St. Petersburg, 1992), 176.

54. *Obzor* 6 (January 1–July 1, 1883), 30–33; also *Byloe*, no. 8 (August 1906), 162–63.

55. *Obzor* 7 (July 1, 1883–January 1, 1884), 27–29.

56. Ibid., 8.

57. M. Ashenbrenner, in *Byloe*, no. 7 (July 1906), 13.

58. *Obzor* 7 (July 1, 1883–January 1, 1884), 6.

59. Ibid., 8.

60. Dmitrii Kuzmin, *Narodovol'cheskaia zhurnalistika* (Moscow, 1930), 119.

61. *Obzor* 5 (September 1, 1882–January 1, 1883), 24.

62. On Kaliuzhnaia, see Figner, *Trud*, 352.

63. *Obzor* 5 (September 1, 1882–January 1, 1883), 25, has biographical information on Surovtsev.

64. Figner, *Trud*, 353.

65. *Golos Moskvy*, no. 46 (February 26, 1909).

66. GARF, Fond 102, 7 DP, D. 747, ch. 12, t. 2, list 23v.

67. *Obzor* 5 (September 1, 1882–January 1, 1883), 23–30, has the official police report on the seizure of the Odessa printing press.

68. *Nasha Gazeta*, February 13, 1909.

69. Kucharzewski, *Od bialego caratu*, 142.

70. *Golos Moskvy*, no. 46 (February 26), 1909.

71. Ibid. See also Tikhomirov, "Neizdannye," 169.

72. *KA*, no. 5/30 (1928), 163.

73. Figner, *Trud*, 354.

74. Kuzmin, *Narodovol'cheskaia zhurnalistika*, 119.

75. Tikhomirov, "Neizdannye," 169.

76. *Byloe*, no. 8 (1906), 267.

FOUR

The Police Run the Revolution

1. GARF, Fond 102, 3 DP, 1882, delo 782.

2. The police response is in GARF Fond 109, 3 Eksp., 1880, opis' 165,

delo 786. See further Jonathan W. Daly, *Autocracy Under Siege* (De Kalb, Ill., 1998), 59–60.

3. Peregudova, *Politicheskii sysk,* 116–18, 377–80; V. Ia. Bogucharskii, *Iz istorii politicheskoi bor'by v 70-kh i 80-kh gg. XIX veka* (Moscow, 1912), 96–97n.

4. Peregudova, *Politicheskii sysk,* 118, 379–80.

5. Quoted in P. S. Ivanovskaia, *V Boevoi Organizatsii: Vospominaniia* (Moscow, 1929), 142.

6. *NChS* 9 (1925), 214.

7. F[eliks] Lure, *Politseiskie i provokatory* (St. Petersburg, 1992), 190.

8. Norman M. Naimark, *Terrorists and Social Democrats* (Cambridge, Mass., 1983), 19.

9. Tikhomirov, "V mire," 95.

10. Ibid., 94.

11. Plehve's assurance: Ludwig Kulczycki, *Geschichte der russischen Revolution* (Gotha, 1911), 2: 467.

12. *Sotsialist-Revoliutsioner,* no. 2 (1910), 106–7.

13. Kucharzewski, *Od bialego caratu,* 142–43.

14. E. A. Serebriakov, in *Byloe,* no. 4/16 (April 1907), 112.

15. N. S. Rusanov, *V emigratsii* (Moscow, 1929), 120.

16. M. P. Shebalin, *Letuchaia tipografiia "Narodnoi Voli" v 1883 g.* (Moscow, 1926), 24.

17. *Byloe,* no. 8 (1906), 265–72.

18. Tikhomirov, "Neizdannye"; Dmitrii Kuzmin, *Narodovol'cheskaia zhurnalistika* (Moscow, 1930), 135.

19. See Appendix.

20. M. Ashenbrenner in *Byloe,* no. 7 (July, 1906), 13.

21. Tikhomirov, "Neizdannye," 170.

22. *Obzor* 7 (July 1, 1883–January 1, 1884), 12–13.

23. A. A. Spandoni, in *Byloe,* no. 5 (May 1906), 20–21.

24. GARF, Fond 102, 3 DP, 1884, no. 1028, ch. 1, list 38. A second, more detailed report, dated January 15, 1883, is ibid., list 39.

25. Figner, *Trud,* 355–56.

26. Kucharzewski, *Od bialego caratu,* 149–50.

27. V. D. Novitskii, in *Sotsialist-Revoliutsioner,* no. 2 (1920), 105–6.

28. *Narodovol'tsy 80-kh i 90-kh godov* (Moscow, 1929), 57.

29. I. I. Popov, cited in M. P. Shebalin, *Klochki vospominanii* (Moscow, 1935), 329.
30. One such list is available in GARF, Fond 102, 3 DP, 1884, delo 208, lista 2–36.
31. Figner, *Trud*, 369.
32. S. S. Volk, *Narodnaia Volia* (Moscow, 1966), 148; V. I. Chuiko in *Narodovol'tsy*, Sbornik III (Moscow, 1931), 185.
33. Kucharzewski, *Od bialego caratu*, 152; Volk, *Narodnaia Volia*, 145.
34. Lev Tikhomirov, *Pochemu ia perestal byt' revoliutsionerom* (Moscow, 1895), 40.
35. V. I. Sukhomlin in *KiS*, no. 24 (1926), 87.
36. German Lopatin, in *NChS* 9 (1925), 217n; Tikhomirov confirms: "Neizdannye," 168.
37. GARF Fond 102, 3 DP, 1884, delo 834, list 157.
38. A. P. Pribyleva-Korba, *Narodnaia Volia* (Moscow, 1926), 174.
39. N. P. Makletsova (Degaeva), in *Byloe*, no. 8 (August 1906), 270.
40. Tikhomirov, "Neizdannye," 165.
41. Ibid., 168.
42. Ibid.
43. Lure, *Politseiskie*, 198–99, referring to Ivan Ivanovich Popov, *Petr Filippovich Iakubovich* (Moscow, 1930), 113.
44. Vasily Karaulov, in *NChS* 9 (1925), 214, 217.
45. Kuzmin, *Narodovol'cheskaia Zhurnalistika*, 134–56.
46. Shebalin, *Letuchaia tipografiia*, 16.
47. Karaulov, in *NChS* 9 (1925), 216.
48. D. Zaslavskii, in *Byloe*, no. 25 (1924), 91.
49. *Literatura Partii "Narodnaia Volia"* (Moscow, 1930), 198–200, under the title "Concerning Jewish Disturbances."
50. Bogucharskii, *Iz istorii politicheskoi bor'by*, 218–30, gives examples of such anti-Semitic exhortations in the revolutionary press.
51. Ibid., 224–25.
52. V. Tsederbaum, *Partiia "Narodnaia Volia"* (Moscow-Leningrad, 1928), 182.
53. German Lopatin, cited in Shebalin, *Klochki*, 324. The spurious Executive Committee consisted of Degaev, the Karaulov brothers, Vasily and Nikolai, Petr Iakubovich, and Sophia Usova.

54. Tikhomirov, "Neizdannye," 171.

55. *KA*, no. 5/36 (1929), 130.

56. Spandoni, in *Byloe*, no. 5 (May 1906), 28–29.

57. *KA*, no. 6/31 (1928), 114.

58. Tikhomirov, "Neizdannye," 95.

59. *KiS*, no. 24 (1926), 160.

60. Tikhomirov, "V mire," 97.

61. *NChS* 9 (1925), 216.

62. Ibid.

63. Ibid., 215.

64. GARF, Fond 102, 3 DP, 1884, delo 834, list 20.

65. Tikhomirov, "V mire," 98.

66. *Dnevnik gosudarstvennogo sekretaria A.A. Polovtsova: 1883–1892*, I (Moscow, 1966), 157.

67. *The Times*, January 9, 1884, 5.

68. *NChS* 9 (1925), 211.

69. A. A. Shilov, ed., *German Aleksandrovich Lopatin* (Petrograd, 1922), 14.

70. Shebalin, *Klochki*, 324.

71. Ibid.

72. Museum of Revolution, Moscow, Fond 9104, opis' 1, delo 1. Also *Sovremennik*, no. 1 for 1911, 401.

FIVE

Sudeikin's Murder

1. S. Valk, in *KA*, no. 5/36 (1929), 124; Kucharzewski, *Od bialego caratu*, 312; M. P. Shebalin, *Klochki vospominanii* (Moscow, 1935), 151–52.

2. Valk, in *KA*, 24–25; S. S. Volk, *Narodnaia volia* (Moscow-Leningrad, 1966), 150.

3. Shebalin, *Klochki*, 150.

4. *Sotsialist-Revoliutsioner*, no. 2 (1910), 104.

5. F[eliks] Lure, *Politseiskie i provokatory* (St. Petersburg, 1992), 203.

6. GARF, Fond 102, 3 DP, 1884, delo 834, list 154.

7. *Obzor* 7 (July 1, 1883–January 1, 1884), 18.

8. Ibid. The attacks on the Kharkov post office on October 17 and October 24 are reported in *KA*, no. 6/31 (1928), 115.

9. GARF, Fond 102, 3 DP, 1886, delo 814, list 1.

10. Ibid., 6–6v.

11. *NChS* 9 (1925), 213.

12. Testimony of Starodvorskii, ibid., 210–11.

13. GARF, Fond 102, DP 7, opis' 1884, delo 417, ch. 2, list 378.

14. *NChS*, ix (1925), 213.

15. GARF, Fond 102, DP 7, opis' 1884, delo 417, ch. 2, lista 377v–78.

16. N. Makletsova-Degaeva, in *Byloe*, no. 8 (August 1906), 270.

17. *NChS* 9 (1925), 205–18.

18. Ibid., 210.

19. M. P. Shebalin, *Letuchaia tipografiia "Narodnoi Voli" v 1883 g.* (Moscow, 1926), 27.

20. *Byloe*, no. 4 (1906), 22.

21. Ibid., 20.

22. Makletsova-Degaeva, in *Byloe*, no. 8 (August 1906), 272.

23. *Literatura Partii "Narodnaia Volia"* (Moscow, 1930), 211.

24. Boris Sapir, ed., *Lavrov: Gody Emigratsii* (Dordrecht, 1974), 1: 587–88.

25. *Byloe*, no. 4 (1906), 22–23.

26. Feliks Kon, *Vospominaniia* (Moscow, 1935), 38.

27. Ibid., 38; GARF, Fond 102, DP 7, opis' 1884, delo 417, ch. 2, list 378v.

28. *Byloe*, no. 8 (1906), 272.

29. N. M. Salova in *Granat*, vol. 40, 403.

30. Ibid.; Lure, *Politseiskie*, 211.

31. *"Narodnaia Volia"—Degaevshchina—Protsess 14-ti* (St. Petersburg, 1907), 44.

32. GARF Fond 102, 3 DP, 1884, delo 834, lista 163–64.

33. *"Narodnaia Volia"—Degaevshchina,* 44; Salova in *Granat*, vol. 40, 403. See further, appendix.

34. Sapir, *Lavrov,* 1: 588.

35. Report by head of St. Petersburg Gendarme Administration to the Department of Police, dated December 24, 1883: GARF, Fond 102, 7 DP, 1883, delo 1309, lista 22–25.

36. Sapir, *Lavrov,* 1: 588.

37. *The Times,* January 9, 1884, 5.

38. P. A. Valuev, *Dnevnik, 1877–1884* (Petrograd, 1919), 246.

39. *K. P. Pobedonostsev i ego korrespondenty,* vol. 1, part 1 (Moscow, 1923), 326.

40. Norman M. Naimark, *Terrorists and Social Democrats* (Cambridge, Mass., 1983), 20.
41. Nikolaevsky Archive, Hoover Institution, box 203, folder 30.
42. *Novoe Vremia,* no. 2807 (December 20, 1883), 3, and no. 2812 (December 25, 1883), 5.
43. *Moskovskie Vedomosti,* no. 350 (December 21, 1883).
44. *The Times,* March 1, 1884, 7.
45. See illustration on p. 112.
46. Makletsova-Degaeva in *Byloe,* no. 8 (August 1906), 271.
47. Sapir, *Lavrov,* 2: 151–52.
48. Sapir, *Lavrov,* 1: 589.
49. Translated in *Obshchee Delo,* no. 58 (1884), 13.
50. *Literatura Partii "Narodnaia Volia"* (Moscow, 1930), 211.
51. Ibid., 224.
52. GARF, Fond 102, 3 DP, 1884, delo 39, ch. 1, lista 14–15.
53. M. N. Polonska-Oshanina in *Byloe,* no. 6/18 (June 1907), 10.
54. N. M. Salova in *Granat,* vol. 40, 402.
55. *Golos Moskvy,* no. 53 (March 6, 1909).
56. Sapir, *Lavrov,* 2: 149–50.
57. Ibid., 150–51.
58. *To-Day* 2 (new series), no. 12 (London, 1884), 602.
59. Degaev refers to an article in *Narodnaia Volia,* no. 10 (September 1884), "From the Executive Committee of the People's Will Party," reproduced in the appendix.
60. Sapir, *Lavrov,* 2: 154–55.
61. *Vospominaniia L'va Tikhomirova* (Moscow, 1927), entry dated January 20, 1885.
62. Hardesty and Unruh, 13–14.

Epilogue

1. Hardesty and Unruh, 17.
2. F[eliks] Lure, *Politseiskie i provokatory* (St. Petersburg, 1992), 212; *Poslednie Novosti* (Paris), February 15, 1934.
3. *Golos Moskvy,* no. 45 (February 25, 1909).
4. L. G. Deich, *Provokatory i terror: Vospominaniia* (Tula, 1926), 28–30.
5. *Svoboda Rossii,* no. 13 (April 26, 1918), 3.

6. I. Genkin in *KiS*, no. 9 (1933), 135.

7. Olarovskii, the Russian consul general in New York, reported on Russian émigrés; Peregudova, *Sysk*, 144, 167.

8. GARF Fond 102, 3 DP, opis' 1884, no. 1028, chast' 1.

9. "Nezavisymyi," in *Utro Rossii*, April 21, 1913.

10. N. P. Makletsova-Degaeva in *Byloe*, no. 8 (August 1906), 265–72.

11. GARF Fond 102, 3 DP, 1886, delo 814, lista 66–66v.

12. *Vospominaniia L'va Tikhomirova* (Moscow, 1927), 231–35.

13. *Pochemu ia perestal byt' revoliutsionerom* (Moscow, 1895), 14.

14. Figner, *Trud*, 358.

15. V. Ia. Bogucharskii, *Iz istorii politicheskoi bor'by v 70-kh i 80-kh gg. XIX veka* (Moscow, 1912), 100.

16. V. Burtsev, *Za sto let* (London, 1897), 2: 130.

17. Lure, *Politseiskie*, 214.

18. V. Burtsev, *Bor'ba za svobodnuiu Rossiiu: Moi vospominaniia (1882–1922)* (Berlin, 1923), 1: chapters 36–45; Deich, *Provokatory*, 31.

19. German Lopatin, in *Byloe* (April 1907), 298; Peregudova, *Sysk*, 141.

20. *KA*, no. 5/36 (1929), 164.

21. GARF, Fond 102, 3 DP, 1884, delo 834, lista, 149–50, 154–55, 162–63.

22. *KA*, no. 5/36 (1929), 168.

23. G. Golovkov and S. Burin, *Kantselariia nepronitsaemoi t'my* (Moscow, 1994), 56.

24. Petr Ryss, *Portrety* (Paris, 1928), no pagination, chapter on A. M. Kalmykova.

Index

CPSIA information can be obtained at www.ICGtesting.com
Printed in the USA
LVOW062332180512

282378LV00001B/5/P